Unwelcome:

50 Ways Churches Drive Away First-Time Visitors

By Jonathan Malm

Foreword by Kem Meyer

ISBN-13:
978-1502355966

ISBN-10:
1502355965

Published by the Center for Church Communication
Los Angeles, California
www.CFCCLabs.org

Cover design by Joe Cavazos.

*To every church that opens
their doors to new guests.*

Contents

Foreword by Kem Meyer
Introduction

First Impressions

Worship

Programming

Communication

The Big Picture

Foreword

by Kem Meyer

Going to a new place the first time can be scary. Think about your first day in a new classroom, the first time meeting your date's parents, your first day on the new job... major butterflies. But the first time you go to a new church? The scariest.

Where do you go? What do they want? How long are they going to keep you here? Are they weird? Should you stand up? Sit down? Hug? Kiss? Run? Walk? There are so many horror stories playing out in your brain. There's a lot you don't know. But there's one thing you can count on: anxiety.

Anyone who walks in the front door of a new church the first time—even the most seasoned "church person" —can't help but be overwhelmed by the experience. It's easy to be skeptical or guarded. It's more complex than we realize. People aren't just learning their way around a new building. They're learning their way around new people, new rituals, new expectations and maybe even a new life. That learning curve is scary!

You made it out alive...

When the first visit is all over, will you be relieved? Will you bolt for the door, never to return? Or will the church you chose to visit have gone the extra mile to ease all this anxiety?

That's the real question. Because catering to first-time guests isn't about consumerism and appealing to felt needs. It's courtesy. We make this harder on ourselves and harder on our guests. But it's really simple: A good host takes care of their guests and puts them at ease. You welcome them. It's no different for a church.

And, yet, it's just so easy to use our spirituality as an excuse to abdicate our responsibility. Isn't it? Why do we think our holy intentions disqualify our shortcomings? That's not on God. It's on us. It's our job to sort it out and face the reality about how we're coming across to others. If we're not intentional about it, then guests will feel unwelcome in our churches.

The problem is that what's glaringly cringe-worthy to others is invisible to us.

Call for backup...
You can't see the whole picture when you're standing inside the frame. You're going to need help. Get perspective from someone who sees the world differently than you.

- When you're selling a home you hire an inspector. They check every nook and cranny, so you know what problems need to be addressed. So you can be ready before potential buyers come with their careful and well-justified scrutiny.
- Corporations hire auditors to go through their books and make sure everything is ship-shape. It can save the CEO from jail

time and keep the company from going under. Companies need to find problems and fix them, and the auditor makes it happen.

- You're supposed to go to the doctor every year for a physical. The annual check-up is a good way to see where your body is at, what's changed since the last time, and if you need to be taking new vitamins or getting more exercise.

This book is all of those things. It's a check-up, an audit and an inspection. It's a pro-active way to make sure your church is doing everything you can to make first-time guests feel welcome.

So get going. Use this book as your checklist. It's easy to digest—no doctorate level theology to wade through. Just common sense. And it's easy to implement—no pricey systems you need to rush out and buy. Courtesy is easy on the budget. See your church environment through someone else's eyes and make the necessary improvements.

Going to a new church will always be scary. We can't control that. But we can control how long guests feel scared. We can be awkward and self-involved and keep our guests feeling scared—or at least on edge—for the entire service. Or we can fix our issues, be more welcoming, and help that fear disappear as soon as they walk in the door.

One approach will send people out the door, never to return.

One approach will bring people back, to hear how much they matter to God.

Kem Meyer is a recovering corporate spin doctor who used to think church was for out-of-touch people who just needed to "get a life." She served in communications at Granger Community Church for 12 years—ultimately as the communications director—and is the author of *Less Clutter. Less Noise: Beyond Bulletins, Brochures and Bake Sales.*

Web: KemMeyer.com
Twitter: @KemMeyer

Introduction

There's a controversy spreading around the church nowadays. It's over consumerism in churches.

There are some on one side of the debate who tailor their churches for guests and try to give their community what it's looking for in a church. Then there are those on the other side who say church is a place for Christians. We don't need to try to make it "seeker friendly," because it is a gathering of believers—not an outreach to unbelievers.

This book is not about that controversy. We aren't going there. Instead, we want to talk about things churches do to turn away their guests. These are things we do—completely outside the realm of biblical ministry—that cause guests to shy away from re-entering our buildings.

In Acts 15, the early church was considering the problem of gentiles. There were so many gentiles coming to know Jesus, and the Christian Jews didn't know how to handle it. Some were saying the gentiles needed to be circumcised to be saved. Others disagreed. In verse 19, you hear the conclusion to the whole debate:

"It is my judgment, therefore, that we should not make it difficult for the Gentiles who are turning to God."

Ultimately, this rationale won the argument: **Why should we make it harder for people than it needs to be?**

The 50 "turn-offs" in this book aren't about consumerism in the church. They're little things we do that make it awkward. Or they perpetuate a scary experience for our guests—believers and non-believers—that make it harder for them than it needs to be.

When was the last time you visited a new church? Did you experience the anxiety of going to a new place? Were you worried about whether or not the people there would judge you or that you would stick out like a sore thumb? Were you curious whether or not there would be people in the church like you? Did you know where to park, where to walk, where to sit, etc.?

There's so much that's scary about going to a new place. And sometimes there are simple barriers we accidentally put up that keep guests from feeling welcomed and at home in our churches. No, this isn't about consumerism. It's about courtesy—about hosting the people God sends to our churches. It's about caring for them and loving them enough to remove the barriers that might scare them away or make them feel uncomfortable.

The gospel isn't easy. It calls us to die to ourselves daily. We must pick up our cross and follow Jesus. We must turn over the control of our lives to God. That's hard enough. Why would we make it harder for people to come to our churches than is necessary?

Let's explore these ideas and figure out how we can change a first-time church experience to make it more welcoming.

First Impressions

Chapter 1

The Locked Door

A few weeks ago, my dad visited a new church. After parking, the beautiful main entrance to the church was quite a walk away. But right in front of him were three doors. It was a hot South Texas day. He thought to himself, "Let's get inside as soon as possible. Then we can figure out how to get to the sanctuary."

Door number 1: Locked.
Door number 2: Locked.
Door number 3: Still no winner.

He finally had to backtrack toward the impressive looking entrance—now on the other side of the building—secretly hoping no one saw his antics from inside the nice, cool building.

Churches are places where you're looking to belong. They're filled with future friends and fellow worshipers. It's a horrible feeling to start out looking like a fool.

That's why, as much as possible, you should avoid locked doors. Even if it isn't the main entrance, people expect doors to be open. They expect any door that leads to where they want to go to be unlocked.

It's easy to think everyone approaches your

church from the same direction. I worked at a church that had one set of doors that was actually hard to get to. You had to walk past the clearly marked entrance to the worship center to even get to these doors. To make sure they didn't get left unlocked—since they were never used—we got into the habit of leaving them locked. Surely no one would use these doors.

But I frequently saw people attempt to open these glass doors. I'm even ashamed to admit that a few times, when I saw people approaching these doors, I ducked into my office to avoid the awkwardness of seeing them pull on a locked door.

We eventually figured out there was no reason to keep those doors locked. And we made it part of our morning routine to unlock every door in the building—even the ones we didn't think anyone would use.

Obviously, the exception to this rule is areas where people hope the doors are locked for safety or security purposes—private offices or certain areas where children are.

If you must lock doors, use appropriate signage or place a greeter nearby to keep people from using that door. It may seem like an unnecessary precaution at times, but by doing this you're showing your guests you care about them. You're removing possible barriers so they can receive as much as possible from your service.

Unlocking doors is a gesture of love. Who'd have thought?

Chapter 2

The Signs

How do I get in? Where are the restrooms? Where do I drop off my kids? These are the big questions guests ask when they drive up to your building.

It's important your guests ask these questions. The answers could mean the difference between walking into the worship center or a broom closet. I don't care how beautiful your broom closets are, you probably don't want your guests to enjoy the worship service from there. And you certainly don't want them thinking those are your state-of-the-art nursery facilities.

You know where everything is. You could probably get around your church blindfolded. Visitors can't. It's so easy to forget the sensory overload that can come from being in a new place.

Let's try an experiment. Close your eyes. Draw a mental map of your church facilities. Is it pretty accurate?

Now realize, if you asked a guest to draw a mental map—even a guest who's been to your service a couple of times—they'll draw a blank. Beyond the parking lot and the outside of the building, the inner workings of your church are a mystery to them.

When I visit a church, I can generally find the main entrance and the restrooms, simply because I have a fairly strong grasp on the way churches work. I actually pride myself on being able to anticipate what's around the corner. I know when I'll likely encounter a visitor's kiosk or a coffee shop. But I'm an insider. I know what a sanctuary is. I even know what an undercroft is (churchy lingo for 'basement'). Most guests aren't as churched as me. And they certainly aren't as familiar with your facilities as you are.

My brother used to work for an airline and got frustrated with how dumb people appeared. Someone would approach him and ask where the bathroom was. He would point up. They were standing under a huge sign with an arrow that said, in three languages, "Restrooms." People aren't idiots (OK, some are). But when you are in a new place, there can be so many things coming at you all at once you can easily get overloaded.

So your signs need to be large and easily visible. In an attempt to make everything look nice and neat we often color coordinate our signs to blend in with the décor. But when they blend in, we may as well camouflage them in a duck blind. The idea is for a sign to be visible—*easily* visible—and not blend in with the background. A great sign might actually be ugly. But an ugly sign that keeps me from walking into the "Nursing Mothers" room is my best friend. How awkward!

And signs need to use terminology that makes sense. A sign to the "Cross Training Area" does me no good unless I happen to know "Cross Training" is the name of your youth group ministry. Otherwise, it sounds like a gym.

I've been around churches since I was born—even before. So you won't confuse me with a sign to the "narthex." But for the average person, that sounds like a creature from a Dr. Seuss book. So make your signs visible and understandable.

Be generous with your signage. Let people know where to park. Let them know where to enter. Where the restrooms are. Where to check their kids in. Anywhere you can possibly guess a visitor will go, make signage that directs them around. Put it at eye level and make it clear and bright.

A great idea is to have some friends who aren't familiar with your facilities try to find their way around. If they're able to get around naturally and easily, you're doing a great job with your signage. But if you identify a few areas where your friends get lost, beef up the signs in those areas. Maybe tweak the sign's location, appearance or size. You can also train ushers and other greeters when they are saying goodbye to guests to ask if they were able to find everything OK.

Reduce your guests' anxiety over visiting your church by making it easy and natural for them to get around and find the places they need to go.

Chapter 3

The Too Welcome

Can a church be too friendly or welcoming?

One person's friendly is another person's cold and yet another person's smothering. People have different standards when it comes to feeling loved and welcomed in a new place. Different cultures expect different things. Different genders expect different things.

This issue is very contextual. But let me tell you a story as we explore this topic.

I walked into a church in the Northeast. It was a smaller church and it looked fairly traditional. An older white woman immediately greeted me. She was very sweet and gracious. She shook my hand. Great. Then she proceeded to bring me in for a hug. Less comfortable, but she's a sweet grandma. How could I be too upset about that? But then she put her cheek to mine. That was the limit of my bubble. That was too close.

Besides the fact that it was a full-frontal hug—not a side hug—I also just met her. We hadn't even exchanged names. The hug with the cheek touching was too much. I don't care how clean she was or how nice she smelled. That was too much contact for my first interaction at the church.

I'd even venture to say that hugging your first-time guests is too far as well.

Some people have bubbles they don't want popped. Some might be worried about their hair getting messed up—or falling off. Some might be concerned their breath smells bad. Some might even be dealing with phobias or baggage that keeps them from wanting too much interaction from strangers. Give your guests space when you first meet them.

I'd suggest instructing your greeters to offer a handshake at most. And even then, that should be on a case-by-case basis. Some people don't want to shake hands. They're nervous. Their palms are sweaty. They want to get whatever bulletin or piece of literature they're required to grab and find their seat. They're on a mission to find comfort, and when you stop them and pop their personal bubble, you make them feel more self-conscious than they are already feeling.

Learn to identify guests who want interaction and guests who want to be left alone. A good rule of thumb is eye contact. If a guest makes eye contact with a greeter, there's a good chance they want a bit of interaction. But if a guest doesn't sustain eye contact, they want to be left alone. I almost guarantee it. Wait until the end of the service or until they're in their seat before being too friendly.

Can a church be too friendly? No. But greeters can cross personal boundaries and make their guests feel uncomfortable.

Be extremely friendly. Be extremely inviting. But give your guests their space when they need it.

Chapter 4

The Lobby

A church that loves to hang out and chat is a great thing. It's a good sign when your congregation enjoys talking to each other and milling around before the service.

Unfortunately, it can be scary for a guest to enter a packed lobby filled with loud chatter—especially when the entrance to the worship center or another needed location is blocked. It's intimidating for guests to approach complete strangers and ask them to move aside so they can get to the restrooms.

A packed room can provide such great energy. But it can also feel overwhelming for your guests. It's like walking into a herd of cattle—you're always a little worried a stampede might start, and you'll get caught in the dead center of it all. And that's a bad way to start your Sunday morning services.

If you have an over-filled lobby, you need to make more room. Since most of us can't afford to extend our building into the parking lot, you only have a few options.

One option might be to place incentives in other locations to encourage folks to hang out there—such as donuts in a fellowship hall or nice music and fun visuals in your worship center. People

Unwelcome

hang out where it feels comfortable to hang out. So make other locations comfortable. Don't be too rigid and shove people out of your lobby to keep it from getting too full. But be wise and find ways to loosen up the space.

On the other hand, it can be a strange feeling to enter a lobby of a church whose service starts in a few minutes, and feel like you're walking into a deserted wasteland. Watching a tumbleweed roll across the lobby floor presents a bad omen for what sort of service you're about to experience. You might think, "Did I miss the memo? Is there a reason this place is empty? Maybe I should slip out and head back to my car before it's too late."

If your lobby is completely empty, you might consider placing incentives there to encourage people to stick around. You could put coffee or donuts there. You could set up bistro tables. Make it a place where people feel comfortable milling around and chatting.

Also, make sure you have some greeters in your lobby. They'll naturally attract other people. People like to be where people are. (As long as those people don't turn into a pulsing, menacing crowd.)

Chapter 5

The Full Parking Lot

Our ushers reported a problem. They saw several cars pull into the left turn lane to turn into our parking lot, pause and then drive off. What was up? There were plenty of empty parking spots, but they were all on the backside of our parking lot. From the street, it looked like our lot was packed. Even though we had available parking, our guests weren't seeing the spots and were leaving. They assumed we didn't have room for them.

Most people know the rule that says your church will never grow beyond 80% of your seating capacity. That also applies to your parking capacity. Yes, there are exceptions, but in general your parking lot doesn't have to be 100% full before people turn around and leave—without even stepping foot in your service.

If people don't find a parking spot, they'll leave. What else would you expect them to do? You wouldn't expect them to park on the sidewalk or on the grass. And most people definitely wouldn't park in an adjacent business' parking lot—they don't want to risk getting towed.

In our situation we had spots but needed to make them visible. That's when we developed a parking lot team. Our attendants provided assurance to each car driving into our lot that we had a place for them. They'd actively direct our guests right to a spot and made the whole parking process smoother. Plus, it allowed us to fudge the 80% rule a bit more than normal. We just made sure our parking attendants were right on the ball with their systems.

A happy by-product of the parking lot team was extra smiling faces. As guests drove into our lots, they were greeted by an enthusiastic smile. It added energy and expectation to our services.

Show your guests you love them by making sure they have a place to park. If you've implemented parking lot attendants and are still running out of spaces, you need to think differently. This may mean buying more land. It may mean asking a nearby business for access to their lots on Sundays. Or it may even mean hiring a valet company to help people get a parking spot without having to walk a mile before they reach your front doors.

The parking lot is your guests' first encounter with the church. Make sure they know you want them there by having a space available for them when they arrive.

Chapter 6

The Reserved Parking

Imagine driving up to a business and seeing prime parking spaces reserved for expectant mothers or first-time customers. That would be awesome, right? You'd get the feeling this business really cared about its customers. It's a nice gesture.

Now imagine driving up to a business where the prime parking spot is reserved for the CEO. It paints a bit of a different picture, doesn't it? It seems less like a business built on love for their customers, and more like a business whose whole goal is to serve the whims of the CEO. Even if it's not selfish CEOs behind this idea, they're ultimately responsible. It's their gig. It's their company. They have the power to reserve that spot for special customers or for themselves.

The church isn't called to be a customer service organization. We aren't trying to impress our congregations like they are customers. That's not what we're doing. But if a business can show they love their customers, how much more should we be concerned with showing that we can love our congregation members and first-time guests?

A reserved parking spot for the pastor communicates that everyone serves the pastor, not that the pastor serves the congregation. Letting the greatest among you be the servant to all includes walking a bit farther than everyone else.

I realize there are elements of honor at play here. A church should definitely honor its pastor. But why not get a staff member or volunteer valet to park the pastor's car? While they're at it, why not give it a wash? That's *real* honor. And you still get to show your first-time guests they're important. They're loved.

Generally, you want to avoid telling your guests where they can't park. Except for handicapped parking spots or those reserved for expectant mothers and first-time guests, you shouldn't limit where people can park. The goal of your parking lot is to show people where they *can* park, not where they *can't*. Focusing on this very subtle but important detail can help you show your guests they're cared for from the very first moment they encounter your church.

Chapter 7

The Dirty Church

I worked at a church in an area of the country that had massive cockroach problems. Even though we fumigated enough to kill every living creature within a one-mile radius, it seemed every Sunday a few of the more spiritual of these bugs found their way to our altar for prayer. In fact, they were everywhere and in places you'd never expect.

They were in the hallways, the restrooms, under seats and would even show up a few minutes after you had cleaned. "I just swept this spot, and there's already another one?!"

Cockroaches truly are the only things that will survive a nuclear apocalypse. They're nasty.

When we have guests over to our home, most of us take extra care to make sure things are clean and in order. Why should we treat guests at our church with any less courtesy?

The cleanliness of your church sends a message.

A clean and fresh restroom says we value you, our guest.

Clean windows, dusted furniture and polished floors say we are stewarding the resources God has given us.

A clean children's facility communicates that we love your little ones. They will be healthy, safe and well attended while in our care.

Make sure everything is neat when you open the doors to your guests. But you can't stop there because people tend to make messes. Keep an eye out for those messes and clean them up as they happen during the day.

When people see that you care for your facilities, they'll not only tend to take better care with your space, but they will also more easily believe you'll care for them. You can communicate so much by simply keeping your building clean.

Even if you're losing the battle against cockroaches, you need to keep fighting for the sake of your guests (and you know, general cleanliness). My church ended up calling in a professional exterminator. Every month. It was worth the investment to know our guests wouldn't be surprised by any six-legged greeters.

Chapter 8

The Helpful Greeter

My parents were missionaries in Guatemala where we worked in remote villages nestled on the sides of green mountains. We drove our blue and silver Chevy Suburban all over the country—through tiny villages and over dirt roads.

This was long before cell phones and GPS technology were available to the average person, so we often had to rely on directions from the villagers.

Many times, the people we would ask had no idea how to get where we were going. But Latin American courtesy prohibited them from sending us away without offering some help. So they would point farther down the road and say "recto"—straight ahead. My dad would always try to judge, from the intonations of their voice and quickness of their response, if they really knew what they were talking about or were just making it up to be courteous. Sometimes we would eventually stumble across our destination, and sometimes we ended up on another adventure.

Your church is as foreign to your guests as those remote mountain villages were to us. A pointing hand is nice, but a guide is the best way to go. Don't leave your guests wandering around, wondering if those ushers really knew what they were talking about or if they were just making it up to be courteous.

When you have ushers willing to escort guests to their precise destination, the guests can breathe a sigh of relief. They can relax. They don't have to worry about accidentally entering a restricted area. And they don't have to be concerned with what awaits them when they get there. "Will someone be there to show me where my third grader goes?" Their escort can introduce them, be their advocate and make sure they are well cared for.

Escorting instead of just pointing shows you care. But it also opens a door for another wonderful opportunity. This is a great chance for trained greeters or ushers to talk about what a wonderful church this is. How the church has impacted their family or life. Why the parents can rest assured their children will be well cared for.

It is a chance to make a connection and immediately turn a visitor into a friend. The guest already opened the door for a conversation by asking a question. We just need to train our greeters to step into that opportunity. Train them to go the extra mile (or extra 50 steps). Train them to make a friend while helping someone find their way.

Chapter 9

The Pastor's Dress Code

I had the privilege of working with my dad as he pastored. He hired me as a creative pastor and actually listened to my opinions. I got to have a voice in many of the decisions he made for himself and for the church. It was a wonderful experience.

One thing he didn't budge on, though, was his wardrobe. He refused to wear skinny jeans and sleek shirts. He preferred slacks and a tie. That was a big source of frustration for me.

I just knew if I could force him into tight jeans and update his hairstyle, I could make our church relevant to a younger generation. I knew the right brands would instantly connect with the younger crowd. If he simply dressed like me, we could reach the whole "next generation" community in our city. I was 20. He was 50.

I'm so glad he didn't accept my clothing advice. He probably would've looked ridiculous on the platform. But more than that, he would have *felt* ridiculous. And people quickly pick up on the fact that you feel ridiculous.

When you try too hard to be someone you're not, people see that as being phony. I was trying to turn my dad into a phony—the man people listened to for spiritual advice. What a horrible idea.

You see, the important part of my dad's relevance was his content, not his clothing. No amount of hair gel and denim could make my dad relevant to the congregation. He already was. He was going to reach who he was going to reach. That was the end of the discussion.

You don't necessarily have to dress like someone to reach them. You just have to love them and be willing to listen as well as speak to them.

Don't force your pastor(s) to wear something they aren't comfortable in. They'll be unhappy, you'll be unhappy and so will the congregation. Let your pastors be themselves.

But also realize that people do consider appearance. One of the first things people ask when they enter a church is, "Do people like me attend here?" That includes everything from age, to race, to socio-economic status. We even had folks who said they came to our church because they noticed we had other interracial couples who attended.

Diversity in leadership sends a message that you are a church where all are welcome. When a variety of ages, races and cultures are valued and allowed to serve, you say to guests, "There is a place here for you too."

So while diversity is important, don't stretch reality with a pastoral makeover to achieve it.

Chapter 10

The Reserved Seating

My wife and I decided to check out the Wednesday night service of a church near us. Unfortunately, we arrived one minute late—we had some traffic drama. So we were already in a foul mood. But we were also excited to try the new church.

The first thing to greet us when we entered was row after row of roped-off seats. Being a church savant, I understood the reasoning. This was a low-attended service, and the pastor wanted everyone close. I tend to think this is usually so the pastor doesn't get discouraged, more than to help the people feel connected. But there was no way we could slip in unnoticed as all these nice anonymous seats weren't available to us.

No problem though. There were some nice prime seats at the end of a row. Then we saw "Reserved for Ushers." All the available seats at the end of the rows were reserved. All of them.

Our only option was to start shoulder tapping. "Excuse me, I'm sorry, excuse me." It was obvious these worshippers did not appreciate having their "close encounter" with Jesus interrupted by two latecomers. We snuggled past them and finally got to the empty seats, only to have a finger wagged at us by the folks on the other side of the empty seats. "Sorry, these are reserved for my

Unwelcome

wife and daughter who are coming later."

Ugh. Now we had to backtrack, re-embrace our not-so-friendly new friends at the entrance to the row and continue our search. By the time we finally found our seats, the first song was done and so was our enthusiasm for this new church.

There was no reason it had to go down this way. The simple fix—trained ushers who would have helped us find a seat. They could have done the shoulder tapping and probably would have known Brother Bob always saves those seats for his wife and daughter. We would have felt safe and loved.

Another church I attended during that time was so proactive in their seating protocol that this was never an issue. Instead of waiting until the service started and the church filled up, they proactively seated each guest. They didn't force you to sit anywhere you didn't want to, but they beckoned you to come forward and move further into the row.

Once the service started, you were surrounded by people, which felt great. Plus, if you arrived late, you wouldn't have to walk up to the front of the room to find a seat.

I'm sure when they began this practice they upset a few of their regular attenders. But as a first-time guest and then a regular attender, I loved it. It made me feel secure and kept me from sitting all by myself like the church pariah.

Show your guests you care about them by helping them find a seat. You can't imagine how grateful they'll be. They already navigated the city streets and tried to find the entrance to your building. Tell your guests, "We'll take it from here." Then become their host and guide them where they want to go.

Chapter 11

The Full Service

I once attended a church that was massively popular. There's a reason people loved it so much. They had great worship, great messages and fantastic people who really loved each other.

Unfortunately, that meant their services filled up quickly. In fact, they had to turn people away regularly because their services were at capacity. It was so routine they had signs made up, sitting in the parking lot, ready to be used when the service filled up. They read: "Service is full." They knew they would have to turn people away each Sunday.

What a tragedy. They'd embraced the fact that they didn't want to reach more people. They were happy the size they were. Maybe they didn't consciously think this, but their actions proved it.

They didn't have to do this. They could have started more services. They could have started secondary campuses. They had an overflow room, which was a step in the right direction, but they still had to turn people away. They could have found another overflow room.

The reason I see this as a tragedy is not that this church could have grown larger. That's not the

Unwelcome

45

point of church. But this church was turning away guests. Folks brave enough to try a new church where they knew no one. They got their kids out of bed, helped them find their shoes, drove the 10 minutes, but were turned away because there was no room for them in the inn.

The guest probably would have settled for a stable too, but the answer was still, "No. We don't have a place for you here. Show up earlier next time."

Now, your church might not experience massive growth like this where you have to turn people away. But imagine if, one Sunday, your attendance grew by 15 to 20%. Would you have enough parking spots? Would you have enough seats? Would you have enough volunteers in the kids' area? Or would you have to turn people away?

It's so easy to see the people in your church and tailor your ministry for your current size. It makes sense. But if you're expecting to grow, you can't let the current size of your church determine the capacity of your ministries.

By preparing for this scenario, you're not only stepping up your quality of ministry, but you're also preparing for the real reality that a sermon series you promote might bring in a huge number of people. You're preparing for a huge increase in people visiting your church during Easter. You're preparing for a large family to start attending and bring all their friends with them.

If you're a church filled with life and love, God will send people your way. The question you have to ask yourself is: Have we made room for them so they can come?

Chapter 12

The Empty Service

On a recent flight from India, I was delighted to find some empty seats on the plane. I could stretch out, have some alone time and relax. But what's great on a plane can be a problem in church.

How many services should you plan? One philosophy treats church like the movies. A theater does not wait until one showing is full to add additional showings. You schedule a lot of showings so people can find one that fits their schedule.

This philosophy can be tough on volunteers. You need a lot of them, and they have to be very committed. But it works well if you are simply expecting the congregation to be observers, like they are in a movie.

A second philosophy wants folks to engage—to connect to the worship and to one another. They encourage worshippers to participate and be a part of the event, not just an observer. This is hard to do if I am feeling self-conscious and on display. For me, and I don't think I am that different from most people, it is hard to connect emotionally when you are floating in a sea of empty seats.

My wife and I recently visited a church that had a "participate" approach. They had great worship. They had a great message. It was a beautiful building. But my wife and I were sitting alone in a row, with nobody in front of or behind us. Despite all the encouragement to not just be a spectator, we just couldn't do it. We felt self-conscious standing there all alone. I'm pretty sure nobody was paying attention to us, but it felt like every eye in the place was on these "new folks," and they were all wondering what we were doing in "their church."

The real bummer? They had two services that were both barren like this. If they had combined those two services, it would have been full enough to create the "connect dynamic" they sought, but still with plenty of room to add more people.

I understand they wanted to make room for new people, like I suggested earlier. But too much room can make guests feel awkward.

Two great options: Combine the services. Their volunteers—who worked both services—would feel better utilized. Their staff would have more energy to make their one service even better. And the crowd dynamic would be vibrant. But sometimes a church feels it is important their volunteers are able to attend a service, so two services is a requirement.

In that case, block off sections of the room. This

church could have easily used some pipe and drapes and made the back few rows "disappear." You may just need to rope off some sections. But if you do, make sure you seat people so you don't frustrate them by telling them where they *can't* sit.

A great church brings people closer to God and closer to one another. Relationships grow best when we are together. Schedule your services to facilitate those connections.

Chapter 13

The Late Volunteers

Share a nightmare with me. You agree to a blind date.

You aren't sure who you're meeting. You arrive promptly at the agreed upon restaurant. Your date hasn't arrived, but it's no big deal. You find a table and wait.

Time ticks away. A couple of minutes. Ten minutes. Fifteen minutes seems like an eternity. The waiter comes by and asks if you need anything. He gives you that look of pity. But you have not lost hope... yet. "Did I get the wrong restaurant?" "It was today, wasn't it?" "How can I slip out of here and just disappear?" You feel humiliated.

As you are preparing to make a graceful exit, someone comes over to your table. It's your date. You are relieved but also a little agitated. Not a great way to start a relationship. This person better be totally awesome, or there will definitely not be a second date. They already have some work to do just to get back to zero.

Minus the waiter and romance, this is what a guest experiences when they arrive at your church before a volunteer, greeter or leader.

To be courteous and able to be seated before the service begins, they arrive early at the kid's check-in. But the doors are locked. The "unlocker" is running a few minutes late. "Did I get the wrong time? I don't know what to do, sweetie. Nobody is here."

Or the doors are open but no one is there to help them. "Am I supposed to do this myself? Where do I go? Is there another check-in area I don't know about?"

Or they follow your great signage, find the right classroom, but no one is there. "So do I wait? Is anyone coming? Or do they not have childcare for this service?" When someone does show up there is relief, and they will probably be courteous and not say anything. But they're not likely to come back either. Who wants to repeat that humiliation and awkwardness?

Don't make your first-time guests feel stood up.

Guests often show up early because they don't know what to expect. They don't know how long child check-in takes. And they don't know what traffic will be like. So they often arrive even 15 to 20 minutes early.

Make sure your volunteers are present and ready 30 minutes before start time. You're much more likely to get a "second date" with your guests if you're there when they arrive.

Chapter 14

The Ambient Light

I had the privilege recently of visiting a church that meets in a movie theater.

It was a bright, sunshiny day. I walked up to the theater, was greeted by some fantastic greeters and then entered the building.

They had a cool, dimly lit vibe going on inside. But to my tiny pupils it was pitch black. I couldn't see a thing. Fantastic greeters were chatting it up, handing me things and letting me know how glad they were I was there. It would have been awesome if I could see anybody.

I wanted to escape but had visions of walking into a darkly painted wall. My confusion might have conveyed hostility because the greeters pretty quickly retreated and left me alone.

The service was great and the people were friendly. I ended up loving the church. But my first impression of them (and their first impression of me) was weird due to my "deer in the headlights" entrance.

Like receiving guests at our home, when people come into our church they should feel wanted and welcome. They should sense it's a place they belong, a place they are valued. A place where they can see.

Unwelcome

To do that, we have to be working to break down barriers they have unconsciously erected—barriers designed to "protect" themselves as they venture into a new place. Every second a guest encounters your church should be a second that breaks down these barriers.

This is not about consumerism. You would treat a guest in your home with dignity. Why would you treat a guest in your church with any less respect? Help them come out of their shell so they can experience all God has for them at that time and for eternity.

Be aware of what people see—or don't see—when they move through your facilities. The same thing applies when they transition from foyer to sanctuary. If you have a dark foyer, bring in some lamps or spotlights to brighten things up. Cover dark walls with light banners or fabric. If you have a dark sanctuary, make sure there are aisle lights or ushers are equipped with flashlights to greet and guide folks as they enter.

Let there be light.

Chapter 15

The Question of Children

I think there might be a special imp in hell specifically assigned to hide children's shoes every Saturday night. Why does it seem they can never find them on Sunday morning? Then there are orange juice spills and arguments on the ride to church. You're lucky if you get there a few minutes before church begins, and you still have to get your kid to the children's ministry program.

Imagine trying to do that as a first-time visitor to a new church. What do you do with your kids? Churches need to make parents as comfortable as possible, and that means making children's ministry options clear and painless.

If your church has a separate program for kids, have extra greeters on hand to accompany parents to the classrooms and answer questions along the way.

If your church welcomes kids into the service but has a special kids' program part way through, make sure parents understand how it works. Explain it from the platform or in the bulletin.

If your church either doesn't have kids' programming or saves it for another time, find ways to make kids (and their parents) comfortable during the service. Offer activity bags with crayons and coloring books for younger kids. Have a quiet room ready for crying babies, and make sure it doesn't feel like these beleaguered parents have been banished.

Imagine you're a first-time visitor and you had to wade through all that to figure out what to do with your kids. It gets worse if there's a line at the children's ministry check-in. You're getting anxious. Your kids are getting anxious. They're getting grumpy. You're getting grumpy. They start acting up. You start acting up. It's not pretty.

You finally get to the service, but you're 10 minutes late and completely frustrated.

How much do you think you'll be able to get from that Sunday service? Will you be able to focus on worship? Will you get much from the message? Or will you spend the next hour focusing on getting your blood pressure down to sub-nuclear levels?

Now imagine your child is acting up and the children's ministry leaders need you, so the slide operators put your child's identifier on the screens. It's a slide that covertly says, "Come get your horrible child: Timmy." Of course that would happen today—the most stressful day on planet earth.

I've even been to some churches that use the

child's name on the announcement screens. That's absolutely humiliating.

Don't let this happen to your guests.

If you're a large church and use this big screen notification system for parents, get a check-in process that assigns each child a discrete identification code.

If you're a smaller church that relies on the classic tap on the shoulder, remember to be discreet and friendly. No matter how awful the kid's behavior, no parent wants to be interrupted and embarrassed in the middle of the service by a scowling children's ministry worker whose whisper carries.

Or imagine the worship songs are ending and it's time for the kids to head downstairs for a snack and an age-appropriate lesson. You're relieved your antsy kid won't have to sit through a 45-minute sermon, but you feel that anxiety swell as your out-going kid clams up and refuses to join the others. Every kid in the sanctuary is leaving and not a single adult is going. Should you go with your child to make sure everything is OK? Is that allowed? Or do you stay in the service and shush your kid through the entire sermon?

Don't let your guests suffer through this indecision.

Give parents and kids options, and let them know it's just fine to do whatever they want. Dismiss the kiddos during a song so parents can go with them, everyone can feel more comfortable, and parents can return to the service without missing the beginning of the sermon.

The entire process of sending kids to a children's ministry program—however you do it—needs to fill parents with confidence. If you can make the process painless, you've done something huge to help your guests with children engage in the service. And you've shown you really care for their children, because you care about the processes that protect them.

Sometimes we take security too seriously or not at all. We either set up far too much red tape—making parents wait in line for a detailed and time-consuming check-in process—or we expect parents to willingly send their kids off with strangers without knowing anything.

Find the balance between tangling red tape and scaring parents. Do as much as necessary to make your children's ministry secure and safe, then leave it at that.

Just as Jesus welcomed the little children, churches need to make kids and parents feel safe.

Chapter 16

The Trustworthy Childcare Worker

McDonald's figured it out a long time ago. Parents will go to a place they don't like if it makes their kids happy. Parents will sacrifice for their children.

We can pour our effort into creating a fantastic message, worship service and guest experience for "big church." But if parents don't feel comfortable leaving their kids in the nursery, or if Junior found the children's ministry "boring," it is likely they won't come back. Even if the parents loved everything about the church, loving parents will sacrifice what they prefer to provide the best for their children.

With all the news about missing children, child abuse and sexual exploitation of children, responsible parents would never consider leaving their children alone for an hour or more with a total stranger. But that is exactly what we ask guests to do when we invite them to leave their precious bundles in our nursery or children's ministry.

While background checks give you confidence your workers have a clean history, that's all "back office." Parents are going to decide whether they have confidence in your children's ministry by what they experience when they drop their children off. And that is where many churches fall short without even knowing it.

A secure check-in is helpful and adds confidence. But if they then go to a classroom and find one teenage girl in the room, or worse yet but not uncommon, one teenage girl and a teenage boy, they are naturally going to wonder. "Does this young girl know anything about caring for children? Are they even going to watch my child or spend the next hour flirting?" And shows like *Teen Moms* don't increase people's confidence in teenagers as caretakers.

Remember, these guests don't know you and don't know the people they are turning their children over to. For many, this is a huge step of faith. That's why it's important you work hard to have adults staff your children's ministry. And do your best to not only have qualified and quality people, but also make sure they look like they know what they are doing.

We know God looks at the heart, but people look at the outward appearance. Your guests can only judge by how your people appear. If Mom is constantly worried about the state of her little one, she is not going to enjoy the service no matter how much effort you have poured into creating a wonderful worship experience and unprecedented presentation of the Word.

While the disciples didn't have time for them, Jesus invited the children to come to him. Children's ministry needs to be just that—ministry—not just childcare so you can reach the adults. Show your guests you love them and understand the heart of God for kids by showing you love and care for their children, too.

Chapter 17

The Overlooked Odor

Do you remember when you used to visit your grandparents' house? Do you remember that smell? It was an old smell. Musty. It wasn't particularly bad, but it *was* particularly old smelling.

It's funny how I'll smell something remotely similar to that musty smell, and it immediately takes me back to the way I felt about it when I was a kid. It's the smell of mothballs, Goodwill or sometimes even the old air conditioner in my car. It immediately transports me back to my 5-year-old self, holding my nose, waiting for the visit to be over. It happens because smell is the sense most strongly tied to memory.

I used to work in a church that met in an older building. It was built in the 1970s. Every now and then—and I have no idea why this would happen—the old smell would manifest itself on Sunday mornings.

We worked in the building during the week and the smell was normal. Even pleasant. But on Sunday mornings it seemed to seep out from mysterious cracks and crevices. Was it an evil spirit? I'm not sure. But the smell was there.

It would have been easy to overlook it. It's just

Unwelcome

a smell. But it spoke volumes to people as they entered our building. It told them they'd get an outdated service, and it wouldn't feel like home to them. Instead it brought images of a senior citizen's center or funeral parlor. It wasn't exactly the atmosphere we were going for.

So we didn't overlook it. We got scented candles, spray fragrances… anything to get rid of that smell.

Although our building was just a room, we wanted people to be transported into a new atmosphere when they entered the building. That's why we spent money on lighting, staging and great sound systems. We wanted to captivate their ears and eyes. We wanted them to feel like they walked into something bigger than themselves. And the wrong smells ruined that atmosphere.

What about the restrooms? You know the smell of death that hits when you walk into a restroom after someone has defiled it?

I know it's completely out of your control, but that smell is still in your building. What are you going to do about it? What about your ushers and greeters? A church-provided stash of breath mints and even body spray can be a lifesaver. What do you want guests to remember about your church? Do you want them remembering their dead grandparents or their eyes watering in the restrooms? I'd imagine not.

Care for your guests by caring for the smells in your church.

Chapter 18

The Greeter Gauntlet

Do you remember that TV show from the 1990s, *American Gladiator*? Contestants tried to best a bunch of beefy athletes in various competitions to see who was the superior athlete.

There was one particular event I always loved watching called the gauntlet. The contestants had to run down a narrow path to reach their goal. Between the starting point and the finish line, there were burly athletes who held obstacles and objects to slow the contestants down and keep them from reaching their destination. The contestants had to dodge, duck, juke and fake to make it past the crowd of sweaty gladiators to win the game.

I've visited churches that remind me of the *American Gladiator* gauntlet. I approach the front doors and am immediately met by my first greeter. The eager greeter hands me a bulletin and grabs my hand for a shake. Then I get to the door and another greeter opens the door, again offering me a handshake. Immediately inside the door, another smiling face goes for an embrace. Then there's a small groups coordinator giving me a handout.

I imagine myself as a contestant on *American Gladiator*—spinning and dodging to make it past the greeter obstacles and into the safety of my seat. "I just want to sit down!"

Perhaps I'm being a bit dramatic. Perhaps I'm not.

You *should* have greeters assigned to greet guests and distribute information. I'm not suggesting you forgo that. But too many greeters can exhaust and overwhelm your first-time guests.

You can't control if you have an over-friendly congregation. And that's not a bad thing. People can tell the difference between being greeted by a random congregant or by an official "greeter." (And it doesn't take a shirt or name tag for your guests to make that distinction.) Most people don't mind being greeted by random congregants. But when you see an official greeter, your gut reaction is to feel like you're being sold something. We've all been to enough used car lots or electronics stores to know a "hello" actually means I'm about to be manipulated into spending money.

So how many *official* greeters are enough?

As a general rule, you should have greeters stationed at key decision points. These decision points include doors and hallways that split into multiple directions. Any place your guests might have to make a decision about where to go or what door to enter, you should have a greeter making that decision easy for them. Other than that, leave the pathway clear.

A greeter's role is to make the guest feel welcomed and at home. So when you station them at locations that might cause confusion, you're giving the greeter a chance to make the guest feel at ease. You remove the anxiety of a new location. That's when greeters hit their sweet spot.

But when they become obstacles to getting where you are going, you've created a greeter gauntlet. Get rid of the gauntlet and make it easy for your first-time guests.

Chapter 19

The Cold Congregation

"Holy cow, this church is welcoming!" That's what I thought as I made the transition from parking lot to foyer. The parking lot attendees were eager and happy to welcome me to their church. They showed me exactly where to go so I wouldn't enter the wrong door.

Then there were greeters waiting outside the building to welcome me in and open the door for me. They had massive smiles and cheerful voices. The bulletin they handed me was bright and cheery. And as I made my way through the foyer into the worship center, I knew I had found the perfect church.

But as soon as I made it past all the professionally loving volunteers, I was confronted with ice. There was no more welcoming, warm feeling. The folks in the room gave me looks like, "Who is this guy? Why is he in our church?"

It appears the leadership at the church desperately wanted guests in their service, but the congregation missed the memo.

You can't rely on your guest services volunteers and staff to be the only welcoming force in your congregation. That isn't enough.

Professional greeters have less than half the impact of your normal congregation members. It's the same reason pastors have a harder time inviting someone they meet in a coffee shop to church. They're a pastor—it's their job to get people to come to church. But if a random person invites someone to church, it has much more impact. Their job isn't at stake. There's no deeper motive to the invitation. It's not their job to invite people.

Your greeters' jobs, though, are to welcome people. So it doesn't have nearly as much impact as when a random layperson warmly greets a newcomer.

So how do you transfer the welcoming spirit to the congregation members?

While you can't force your congregation to be welcoming, you can cast vision. You can continually tell your congregation how much your church values guests. Cast the vision that each one of those guests is someone's brother, daughter, mother or father, and they want them to hear about Jesus. Cast the vision of how important a welcoming smile is. And make a big deal of it when you see it being done right.

Whatever you praise in people, they begin to value in themselves. As you praise their welcoming spirit, they'll be eager to develop it and get even better.

You can even praise it from the pulpit. The guests in your congregation don't mind hearing you're working on becoming a more welcoming church. They'll even eagerly join in when they hear you spreading that vision.

A welcoming church starts with the leadership. But it can't end there. It has to seep into every crevice and corner of the church. Make sure your congregation gets that. Make sure they see how important guests are.

Worship

Chapter 20

The Unskilled Worship Band

What happens when you have a band whose skill level is a seven, doing a song that requires the skill level of an eight? You get a negative experience.

I visited a church recently whose band probably ranked a four on a scale from one to 10. They weren't horrible. They played most of the right notes, sang mostly on pitch and had a decent sense for rhythm. I'd say, for a small church, they were a wonderful band.

Unfortunately, they didn't have a great grasp of the concept of time signatures. So when the drummer and bass player started playing a 6/8 song in 4/4, the whole thing sort of fell apart.

Worse, none of the rest of the band was going to abide by the 4/4 rhythms laid down by the drummer and bassist. The pianist and guitarist were sticking to their 6/8 time signatures. For the rest of the song, the vocalists and clapping flip-flopped between the two time signatures.

You could see the discomfort on the musicians' faces, the pastor's face and even on the congregation's face. They plowed through the whole song with nary a sense of resolved rhythm. And when the song was over, an awkward silence fell over the room.

Unwelcome

The worship band wasn't horrible. But they played a song outside their skill level. And everyone experienced the awkwardness. Not only that, the band that ranked as a four in skill level was perceived as a two in everyone's eyes that day. They could have avoided all that by simply scrapping the song at practice and pulling out a different one. Sometimes that's the best thing that can happen at a rehearsal.

It's tempting to hear a song on the radio or on an Israel Houghton album and feel the tug to play it on a Sunday morning. But I urge you, evaluate your band's skill level from an unbiased perspective.

Don't try to climb Mount Everest when you have a difficult time climbing the steps to your third story apartment. That is to say, don't attempt a more difficult song when it takes you two hours of practice to get the usual song list down.

There's a place for trying new songs and expanding the skill level of your team. But that doesn't need to happen on Sunday mornings. Develop your team's skill. Practice together. And there may come a time when you're ready to tackle that new song.

But do your very best to make everything you do on Sunday morning feel natural and easy. When it feels natural and easy to you, worship will feel natural and easy to the congregation.

It's such a great experience to be a part of those types of worship experiences.

Chapter 21

The Projected Lyrics

For churches that project the lyrics on a screen, I've noticed one small thing that can make one church's worship services more engaging than another. This one thing, if done right, will encourage more people to sing. Unfortunately, it's nothing the worship leader can do.

It's up to the slide operator. The projectionist. The lyric typer. Here's the secret to more engaging worship services:

Make sure the song lyrics are up on the screen a couple of seconds before you have to sing them.

Yep, it's that simple. When people know the lyrics before they sing them, they sing more confidently. But if they're unsure of the lyrics, they won't sing until they are. And if that happens enough, they'll often give up singing altogether. Who knew PowerPoint, ProPresenter or EasyWorship could be so vital to a good worship service?

It was funny. When I used to lead worship, I could usually predict how responsive the congregation was going to be based on who I saw behind the computer in the tech booth. If it was one of my A-game slide operators, I knew they'd put the lyrics up proactively, and the congregation would

Unwelcome

be able to sing along. But if it was one of my slower operators, I pretty much resigned myself to being one of the only ones singing the songs that morning.

It was such a point of pain, in fact, that I turned over the role of worship leader to one of my drummers and stepped back to the booth to train the volunteers. I worked with them during rehearsals and on Sundays to make sure the lyrics were there before we actually had to sing them. The jump in response I saw from the congregation from such a small act was amazing.

I encourage you to bring the person who runs your slides into rehearsals with you. Encourage them to learn the songs. Even give them an outline of how you plan to do the song. Just like you'd lead other vocalists to sing the right words, lead your slide operator to project the right words. Teach them musicality. Show them what timing and rhythm would feel best for advancing slides.

When they feel confident in where you're going with the lyrics, they can proactively put them on the screen. So while it's up to the slide operator, as a worship leader, you can make it happen.

You can even encourage your slide operator to change the slide on the last word or two of the line the congregation is singing. People typically read a few words ahead of where they're singing, so those last couple of words on the screen aren't that important.

While this may seem a bit silly, I've seen it work. I've seen, firsthand, how important these little projected images are to how the worship service progresses. Amazing.

Chapter 22

The Bad Attitude

This morning, my electric guitar player showed up late for sound check. He gave me attitude when I asked why he was late. So that erupted into an argument. Now we're both mad at each other.

I should probably kick him off the band for this morning's worship set, but he's so stinking good. And church starts in five minutes. I have no backup. So I guess we'll just be mad at each other until after church. Then we can hammer out our grievances and become friends again.

The pre-service countdown is winding down. Now we need to go on stage and worship God. I'm not feeling it, but it's my job. I wish the opening song were more of an angry song instead of a celebratory song. That would at least allow me to slam my guitar strings without it looking too awkward. But I have to be spiritual. The countdown just reached zero, and now it's time to go on.

I think all worship leaders and worship teams can relate to the above story. Part of working with people means friction and bad attitudes. It happens. But we can't allow that to carry into the service.

We may think people don't notice the tension in the air, but you can always cut it with a knife when this sort of thing happens. There's a certain heaviness you feel in a room when people are mad at each other.

It's impossible to completely eliminate these types of meltdowns from happening before service. But there *are* ways we can keep them from bleeding into the service.

It just requires that hard work of intentional forgiveness and confessing our bad attitudes to God before we go on stage. Get rid of the junk in your attitude and worship God without all the baggage from the arguments or frustrating circumstances. Set your ego aside and forgive everyone.

In 1 Corinthians 11, Paul instructs the church in Corinth to do just that. In fact he goes as far as to say if you haven't forgiven someone and you take the Lord's supper, you sin against the body and blood of Jesus. Wow!

These intangible things speak volumes to your guests and your congregation. People can tell if you're trying to lead them into worship with a bad attitude. Sure, they might not be able to pinpoint the exact problem, but they know something's not right. And that makes for an incredibly uncomfortable worship service.

Realize that what's happening on Sunday mornings is bigger than petty arguments or frustrating personalities. Real things are happening in the hearts of those who worship with us, and it's so much more important than who's right or wrong.

The Public Rebuke

Bad attitudes and arguments are the short-term problems. Those are bad enough. But sometimes we allow problems and discord to fester and grow. Then they become long-term problems that unexpectedly explode and everyone in the room is left wondering what just happened.

Short-term problems are awkward for your congregation and your guests. Long-term problems are worse.

Have you ever been in a service where the worship leader calls out the sound guy in the middle of the service? With a little more edge in his voice than would be normal, he says, "Tom, I need more of myself in the monitor. Can you just give me what I need?" He takes a simple request but adds some bite to it—essentially throwing the sound guy under the bus.

Or you might have seen the pastor struggling to speak with tiny bits of feedback rising occasionally as he delivers his sermon. You can tell his frustration is growing, but then he says, "Come on, guys. Get it together." He just called out the whole production team in front of everyone. He turned all attention on them and made them feel completely stupid.

Each of these stories were simple requests that turned into awkward situations because of underlying discord. And yes, they really did happen.

In both of these stories, everyone knew something wasn't right. They knew the worship leader couldn't hear himself. Or they knew there was feedback. Everyone probably even knew it was the production team's fault. It was a bit uncomfortable for everyone in the room. But once the leader threw the tech team under the bus, it got a whole lot more awkward. Obviously something's been festering for weeks to cause such an explosion.

It's awkward. But worse than that, it causes everyone in the room to feel unsafe. When was the last time you felt safe around someone known for random bouts of rage? And if the guest already felt nervous in a new environment, you've just upped the threat level to red. Those guests are going to go running as soon as the service ends, and they'll never want to return.

Don't let these problems and issues of discord fester. Deal with them. And deal with them on a Monday or Tuesday when there isn't so much at stake—not on a Sunday morning. Take the offending people out to coffee or lunch and hash it out. Besides being a wise thing that will help keep you from blowing up in front of guests, it's the biblical approach. Don't allow a root of bitterness to spring up.

Chapter 24

The Over-Eager Worship Leader

I saw a funny picture posted on Facebook the other day. It wasn't intended to be funny, but I laughed anyway. Someone posted a picture of their church's worship service. In the center of the photo, you had a man who was singing his heart out. Liquid passion in the form of tears streamed down his face. He was *really* feeling the worship service.

Then on either side of him—if you looked a bit closer—you could see his band. They didn't seem to share the sentiment. In fact, they looked like they couldn't wait for the service to be over so they could take a nap.

It looked like the singer in the center downed a few liters of espresso that morning, while the band's cereal was spiked with Valium. I thought it was hilarious.

The worship leader was eager to get people engaged—maybe a bit too eager. I imagine if I was there I might have been a bit intimidated by his fervor. And I've grown up in church my whole life. I'm used to this stuff.

Then when you put that next to the other worship team members who seemed miserable to be there, it made for an odd atmosphere.

When I was a worship leader, my pastor constantly reminded me of this unhappy fact: on stage, you're a leader. You don't have the luxury to worship like you're alone in your prayer closet. You're leading others. You have to be aware of where they are, and then bring them along with you.

This means you might need to tone down your natural fervor. While your tear-soaked face might be the perfect way for you to show God how you love him, it might not be the best thing for a public service. And if you're so introverted and introspective that you look like you just woke up from a nap, you might need to rev yourself up a bit for the worship service.

As servants, we're modeling for others where we want them to go. We're creating a corporate worship journey we want others to join us in.

Does your worship team struggle with too much eagerness? Or more likely, does it struggle from a case of morning grogginess?

Maybe it's time to record your worship service on video and watch it together. Maybe it's time to put a mirror in one of the seats in the congregation and see what you all look like as you lead worship.

Most worship teams simply fail to see what they look like when they lead worship. Give it a look! It might surprise you. You might be doing a wonderful job. Or you might be coming across as a bit too eager or a bit too passive.

Chapter 25

The Energy of the Room

Proverbs 27:14 says, "A loud and cheerful greeting early in the morning will be taken as a curse!" I'm pretty sure when Solomon wrote that proverb he was referring to an early morning church service.

I, like many people, prefer silence until I've had my second cup of coffee each morning. During a normal workweek, it takes me a couple of hours before I'm ready to even meet with people or be pleasant. That's why I enjoy attending the latest possible service on a Sunday morning. It gives me time to become a human being.

But there are those occasions—unhappy occasions—when I have to go to an early service. I try to force a smile and cheery handshakes as I enter the service. I'm still waking up, but I don't want to be a jerk. But then the worship leader, hopped up on Red Bull and Mountain Dew, tries to jolt me from my sleep. I get pretty grumpy. I take that loud and cheerful greeting as a curse.

I'm not saying the service needs to start like a funeral procession. The band shouldn't tip toe around during the service. But there needs to be a bit of slow build up before I'm excited to hear someone greet me too cheerfully and loudly.

Let your early morning congregants ease into the service.

At the same time, though, if the whole worship service matched the way I felt early in the morning, I'd probably fall asleep two minutes in.

Be aware of the energy in your room, but don't conform completely to it. If people are quiet, start to slowly build the energy. If people are somber in response to a tragedy, address the elephant in the room and bring people out of that gloom. Worship leaders are called to be thermostats, not thermometers. Sure, you read the temperature in the room first, but then you change it to where it needs to go.

Don't just match the energy of the room. Have a reasonable goal of where you want to take your congregation during your service. Then lead the room from their current energy level to where you want them to be.

Some days you'll need to lead them to a more moderate place. Sometimes you'll feel them chomping at the bit with energy.

Guests—even though they're brand new to your service—can feel the energy in the room. And when they feel the energy of the room rise, their energy rises with it. But when the energy on stage is massively different than the energy in the room, it can feel forced or manipulated.

We're on this journey together. Let's scale the mountain of worship together.

Chapter 26

The Special Song

When I was younger, my church was desperate for solo singers to sing "special numbers" during the offering. It didn't matter if you couldn't sing. If you were willing, they needed you and threw a microphone in your face. It's just what my church did.

It was great for our small community because we had no hopes of growing. We were content to be our little family and no more.

But if you want to embrace guests and have them stick around, this isn't the best way to do it.

One of my favorite parts about watching *American Idol* is seeing the folks who think they can sing belt out a horrible tune and watching the reactions of the judges. It's so much fun because I can see the horror on the judges' faces. I'm not there, so I don't have to experience that awkwardness. That's what makes it funny.

But I would absolutely hate to take the judges' place and have to smile and nod as this poor individual butchered the song. I'd feel bad for the singer. I'd feel like clapping for them even though I know everyone hated it just as much as me—a pity clap. Nobody likes to give pity claps.

Don't make your guests give a pity clap. Don't make them feel awkward.

Also, don't put a congregation in the position of having to receive pity claps. You can protect your precious people from the embarrassment of showing their less-than-wonderful talents to a large group of people.

My rule of thumb is to avoid "specials" or solos unless you have a particular talent you want to highlight. A "special" is special when it doesn't happen all the time. It's special when it's of fantastic quality. It's special when people actually enjoy the piece and talk about it after the service with fondness.

Audition people. Give people a fair shot to show what they can do. But be willing to say "no" (graciously) when it won't work for the service.

You have such a short time with your people on a Sunday morning. Make sure every minute is excellent. It shows you value your people's time and what you're doing as a church enough to put extra thought and preparation into every element.

Chapter 27

The Invitation to Worship

As a worship leader, there were a few sweet weekends where I was sure I put together the perfect worship set. Every song was stacked perfectly, thematically and musically. They were all my A-listers.

Then all my favorite musicians were joining me on stage—the keyboardist who provided sweet synth backing, the guitarist who could truly shred solos and the drummer who put the obsessive compulsive Animal (the Muppet) to shame.

"People's faces will be melted off with worship," I secretly said to myself.

So you can imagine my frustration when, three songs into the set, I felt like the congregation just wasn't responding. The room felt dead.

Here was my temptation. Out of annoyance, I might say, "Come on guys. We need to worship God together. You guys look like you're at a funeral." Maybe I'd add a joke to break the tension, but it would be a passive aggressive gesture at best.

In my mind, saying something like that would always work. The congregation would snap out of their glumness and would join me in hallelujah

Unwelcome

93

choruses for the rest of the morning.

Unfortunately, the few times I tried this, it never worked. They never once responded the way I hoped they would. It ended up making it more awkward than before.

The reason that response didn't work wasn't because the congregation was rebelling against my leadership. Rather, I was taking authority to say things that weren't mine to say. I wasn't their pastor. I didn't have the right to reprimand them for not worshiping. The edge and passive aggressive tone in my voice weren't adding to my authority either.

Most of my congregation members would forgive me. Many of them even came up to me after service and agreed they just weren't feeling it that morning. They realized they weren't locked in with me. (I had an extremely gracious congregation.)

Unfortunately, I never heard from any of the guests that were there for the first time that morning.

That small snapshot of our church service highlighted a bitter battle between the worship leader and the congregation. Do you think that was a positive first impression? Do you think they saw that exchange as healthy?

No. Instead of realizing it might just be a Sunday with low energy, they assumed the congregation wasn't into worship. Or they assumed the worship leader was a punk kid who yelled at the congregation each Sunday. Regardless, they didn't come back.

Remember: Shepherds lead the sheep. They never drive them. Let's gently love our congregations into worshipping—not chastise them.

Chapter 28

The Awkward Transition

Have you ever listened to a radio station and heard complete silence? If you have, you've probably only heard it once or twice in your life. Radio stations have a rule—absolutely no silence.

If you *have* heard it, you might have heard five seconds of silence at most. But those five seconds felt like an eternity. Radio silence has the power to expand in our mind and seem so much longer and quieter than we ever thought possible. It's a crazy phenomenon.

Part of what makes the radio silence so big is my fear that the radio station doesn't know what's happening. Do they know their mics are muted? Did they forget to hit play on the next track? Is there a problem with the technology they're using?

I believe the same sort of thing happens in churches when there's silence because of an unplanned transition. When you see the band looking at each other—not sure who's supposed to start the next song—it gives you a bit of anxiety. Or when you hear the guitar strings clink as the worship leader awkwardly removes the capo and fastens it to the end of the guitar. Or when the worship leader backs away from the mic, unstraps the guitar, places it on the stand

and straps on a new guitar—then starts tuning and plugging it in.

Those few seconds can feel like an eternity—especially in a very tender moment between songs.

It can also happen in other moments, like when the volunteer reading the day's Bible passage is slow to come to the front. Or the person leading the liturgy didn't mark their place and has to quickly flip pages. Communion can be rife with awkward pauses.

I encourage you to plan your transitions. If you want a moment of silence, instruct your congregation that there should be silence. Don't just let it happen and make your people wonder what's going on.

If you have to change your capo or someone has to set up communion, instruct your keyboardist to play something as you make the transition. If you have to change your guitar, make sure the whole band isn't waiting on you to make the switch. Clearly communicate who's starting each song so you don't get that awkward, "Are you starting the song?" exchange between your band mates. Have the people volunteering in the service or giving special announcements in place and ready to go.

When things aren't rehearsed, awkward transitions happen. So if anything is out of the norm, such as communion, a guest speaker or a youth group skit, expect the transitions to be weird and find ways to smooth them out.

And if something goes wrong, as it inevitably will, roll with it. Have an extra song ready to fill unexpected silence. It's OK to laugh off a flub and keep on moving. If the sermon goes long and you need to do some "liturgical slash and burn" and skip the prayers of the people, go ahead and do it. Just explain what you're doing so anyone following along in the bulletin isn't lost.

When the worship team is comfortable and confident on stage, your congregation will be comfortable and confident. That's a great feeling, both for your congregation and for your guests. Give them confidence they're being taken care of because you put the effort and thought into planning ahead. Plan your transitions.

Programming

Chapter 29

The Tardy Guest

In an ideal world, everyone would arrive 10 to 15 minutes early. They'd pull into their parking spot at 9:45 a.m. They'd greet five people as they walked toward the building. They'd grab some coffee, their bulletin and their seat, and they'd still have five minutes to get settled before the service began. Their hearts would be ready, and as soon as the first chord came from the stage, they'd be standing with hearts raised to heaven.

Unfortunately, that doesn't always happen. We live in the real world. It's a world filled with kids who can't find their shoes, cars whose gas gauges are mysteriously on empty and hairdos that just won't behave. And these sorts of things always seem to happen on Sunday morning when you're doing your best to make it to church on time.

When my dad was pastoring, he asked a friend why he was always late to church. "Sunday is the only day I don't have to rush around in the morning. I take my time and let the family know we will arrive when we arrive." He didn't want to have to yell at his family all morning just to get them to church on time.

Unless the first 10 minutes of your church service are notoriously horrible, most people try to be on time to the service at your church. And usually your first-time guests arrive early because they don't know what to expect.

So when you complain or chastise the congregation when they show up late, you punish people who really do want to be on time. And your guests will sense an unhealthy tension between leadership and the congregation. That's a horrible first impression to make on a first-time guest.

As a child, I went to a small church in a growing town. I don't remember many sermons from my time at the church. But I do remember one specifically. For 40 minutes, the speaker chastised the congregation for showing up late. I'm sure he found some Scripture passages to back up his theology, but it was primarily a rant about how annoyed he gets when people interrupt his time of worship.

Want to know how that church is doing today? They're smaller than ever while other churches in the town are growing. Do you think this might be a reflection of doing things like this from the pulpit? Do you think they drove away some guests that day?

Am I saying you just need to accept that a good chunk of your folks will show up to church late? Perhaps. But that doesn't mean you can't try new, creative ways to encourage folks to show up early.

Maybe you could offer free breakfast foods before your service. Or you could put some of your best material at the beginning of your service. You could have pre-service activities for kids and their parents.

There are countless things you can try that offer an incentive to encourage folks to show up early. But if you complain about or chastise people when they show up late, you're showing frustration. Not love.

If you try to control people's schedules, you'll either make them feel manipulated or guilty. There are things that happen to all of us that keep us from arriving on time. It's real life. You have to make allowance for these things.

In this area, like many others, it's better to try to motivate with positive rewards than negative criticism. Love covers a multitude of sins—even tardiness (1 Peter 4:8). Show love to your guests.

Chapter 30

The Early Start

I didn't think this was the sort of thing you needed to tell a church—not to start the service early. Most churches are lucky if they start on time. Many start late.

But one day I visited a church that began their services three minutes early. I verified—my phone was syncing up with the correct time. They began their service early.

I'm not entirely sure what their motivation was. I can only speculate. But I know the guests entering the room after the service prematurely began felt guilty. Even though they arrived on time, they felt like it wasn't good enough. Forget about the people who had to arrive *late*. They felt even worse.

As I said, I can only speculate as to why they'd begin the service early. There are only two explanations I can think of. Either they were trying to encourage people to get there early, or they were hoping to have more time to infuse energy into their service. I'll address the energy issue now and save the "trying to get people there early" issue for another chapter.

Though I don't agree with starting your service early, I love the motivation behind trying to

Unwelcome

infuse energy into your service. If you can raise the energy of the people in the room before the service even begins, that energy will spread. It's infectious. But it doesn't justify making people feel guilty for showing up on time because the service started early.

If you want to infuse some energy into the beginning of your service, focus on the elements that come before the service. Think about introducing a video that builds excitement—that counts down to the beginning of the service. Or consider bringing an emcee on stage to let people know what they can expect and build up their excitement. You could give the band an upbeat instrumental song to play beforehand.

It's OK to stack things into your service before the official start time. Just make sure they feel like pre-service elements. This is a good litmus test: Are you requiring engagement during the pre-service element? If you're asking for engagement, people will consider it part of the service.

But if you're merely offering entertainment or information, you can use this sort of technique to prime the energy in the room without making people feel guilty.

Chapter 31

The Foreign Language

A healthy church filled with people who love each other can feel a lot like a family. You support each other when you go through tough times. You get excited to see each other every week. You even look forward to eating meals together—Susie Jenkins' casseroles at the potluck dinners, anyone?

When love and mutual respect are in the air, you can feel completely at home with your church family. It's like each Sunday gathering is a family event. This is a very good thing.

And every family has their own set of stories and rituals. Everyone in the family knows about that time Uncle Bob caught a tiny fish the size of a nickel. And even if they don't know the story, they understand Uncle Bob enough to know he probably bragged about it anyways—for days and days. So when someone refers to Uncle Bob's fish, everyone laughs and gets it immediately. It's simple.

Unfortunately, as the family grows, it gets more and more complicated. It gets especially complicated for guests who are unfamiliar with the family dynamics.

Unwelcome

A story from a church stage about "Uncle Bob" might get everyone in the congregation laughing. But your guests will feel like complete outsiders. They don't have the context of the story. They don't know Uncle Bob. And they know they're missing something.

It's important we're careful about using insider language on Sunday mornings. Yes, it's a family gathering. So it's OK to tell a story about Uncle Bob. But it's vital you provide the context. Explain a bit about Uncle Bob, and then tell the whole story. Your regulars won't get upset that you're repeating information they already know. And your guests will feel like they're becoming part of the family.

Insider language includes, but isn't limited to:

- **Acronyms or ministry names** - Many people don't know what AWANA (kids' program) or Revolution (youth) are.
- **People's names** - If someone's supposed to "see Joelle for more information," provide their full name and contact information. Don't assume everyone in your congregation knows who Joelle is—even if they're on staff.
- **Insider sayings or slang** - There may be a memorable quote or word that gets referenced from an event or sermon series.
- **Building or room names** - Most of your guests won't know how to find the Roy G.

Biv Fellowship Hall. And I'm still not sure I know how to identify a narthex.

- **Christianese** - We have a tendency to slip into theological shorthand in church. But "asking Jesus into your heart," "loving people for Christ," "being filled with God's presence," and our other lingo can come across as gibberish to the uninitiated. Clichés don't make something as complicated as communion easier to understand.

Evaluate your use of insider language. You don't need to eliminate it from your vocabulary. But it's very important to remember there are guests in your church who don't have the same background and context as your congregation. Plan what you say with that in mind.

You have the opportunity to invite your first-time guests into the family. If you remember they're there and let them in on the inside jokes, they'll start feeling like part of the family in no time.

The Unhelpful Critic

I've noticed an epidemic spreading among the Christian church. It's a virus of criticism that happens in so many churches. And it's turning people off from both the church and the gospel.

It's easy to criticize other pastors or churches. Their approach to ministry is drastically different than our own. They preach things we don't agree with. They approach ministry with what appears to be sensationalism or untried methods.

I visited a church that had been infected by this virus of criticism. They had a wonderful building, fantastic worship leaders and a solid message. Unfortunately, their pastor peppered criticism throughout his sermon. He was gracious enough to avoid naming names, but he referred to "some churches in town" often enough I knew who he was talking about.

The congregation agreed with their pastor whole-heartedly. They nodded their heads and amen-ed like no tomorrow. But I couldn't feel comfortable. I visited many of the churches he was referring to, and I loved their pastors. I had friends who attended those churches. It broke my heart.

You see, the congregation had already chosen this pastor as their leader. They were his disciples.

Of course they agreed with him. They felt like he was protecting them from heresy and sloppy Christianity.

But I saw it as unnecessary and divisive. I felt discouraged more than anything. Even if I'd wanted to be part of the church, I felt like I'd never live up to the standard the pastor set for his congregation.

I'm not saying you shouldn't confront false doctrines and philosophies in the church. Part of a pastor's job is to teach truth. But we don't need to call out other pastors or ministries. Speak to the issue, not to the person. When you speak about a person directly, you lose the power of your argument by turning it into *ad hominem*. It's dirty debating and people know it.

I'm making it a point in my life to never criticize anyone unless I've sat down with the individual for a meal. Unless I've had a chance to connect with the person's heart, I have no business judging their intentions. Paul says in 1 Thessalonians "to make it your ambition to lead a quiet life: You should mind your own business and work with your hands, just as we told you."

Let's show our guests and our congregations we love them. Let's show we love them by loving other pastors and ministries. Let's build others up instead of tearing them down. "In essentials, unity; in non-essentials, liberty; in all things, charity." (Martin Luther)

Chapter 33

The Not a Normal Sunday

When I worked full time as creative director for my growing church, I used to enjoy brainstorming in creative meetings. My pastor (also my dad) was very supportive. And the worship leader (my brother) did a great job at fueling any crazy ideas I had. Because of this, we tried some pretty abnormal things. Unfortunately, a few of them didn't work out.

Behind closed doors in our meetings, the ideas were perfect. They were hilarious, zany, crazy, awesome... But I didn't ever consider first-time guests in the whole process. And when I found out someone was visiting and I knew our creative element failed, I always found myself saying, "Sorry. It isn't normally like this."

Usually the guests came back to give us another try. They realized we were trying to be creative, and they at least respected that we were willing to attempt new things. But it was unfortunate we weren't able to give them an accurate snapshot of our church on the first shot. They had to give us two and sometimes even three tries before they really saw what our church was like. Many guests won't give it that many tries.

Guests are often willing to give it another shot when they know it was failed creativity. But when

Unwelcome

111

it comes to awkward doctrine, weird practices or strange personalities taking center stage, they're much less likely to come back again.

This happened often in the form of guest speakers and guest worship leaders. We'd frequently invite missionaries or friends of friends to take part in the service. Often, we had no idea whether or not they shared our doctrine or ministerial approach. We took an unhealthy risk and let these guests commandeer the service. And by giving them the reins of the service, we implicitly placed our seal of approval on everything they said or did.

One guest speaker, a retired minister who now attended our church, not only was awkward but also a bit heretical. He decided for his premiere speaking engagement at our church he would do a chalk talk. If you've never experienced a chalk talk, they're quite cool. As you speak, you draw a picture on a large board. The picture illustrates your message and brings a bit of mystery for all the people watching. "What's he drawing?"

The whole experience culminates when the picture is completed. You turn on a black light, and if everything turned out right, a brand new picture glows through the visible one. It's quite a stunning effect.

But our friend... He forgot the right chalks he needed at home. His whole drawing was in

Technicolor pastels, and when he turned the black light on, it was a jumbled mess. Even worse, he didn't talk as he drew. He played some old school calliope music for 20 minutes as he drew his mess of a picture. When the picture failed, he went off script and said some things we didn't agree with—like sin is merely the bad stuff that happens to us.

Our guests saw this man's whacked doctrine and weird personality, and they assumed he represented our church. How unfair that was to our first-time guests and to our own congregation members who invited their friends!

We knew each week our congregation members were working to convince friends and family to come to church with them some Sunday. Imagine the one Sunday their guests showed up, and this happened. That left the inviter embarrassed for putting the invitee in that situation. They had to apologize and assure them they weren't expecting that. We broke trust.

My dad is a pretty flexible guy, and when things went awry he would usually say something like, "At least it was different. And what did it hurt?" It was *this* Sunday that taught him that was the wrong question. When the members of your congregation have spent all their friendship capital to invite a friend, and it turns out to be a disaster—the kind that could have been avoided—it is clear what was hurt. A better question, and one my dad started asking was, "What is this going to do to help—to help our folks reach their family and friends?"

Don't put your congregation in that position. Don't make them say, "We don't normally do this."

Chapter 34

The Pre- and Post-Service Moments

There are a few fairly pivotal moments in your service that also seem to be magnets for awkward silence. The first moment is right before the service starts, and the second moment is right after the service ends.

Before the Service

Some of my most frustrating moments in working at my church were unfortunate timing for the pre-service playlist. This happened way too often. I should have learned from my mistakes the first time. But this is the sort of thing that happened.

With 20 seconds left on our pre-service countdown timer, a song would end on our pre-service mix. This was unfortunate because it's sort of weird to interrupt the intro of a new song—which is what would happen in 20 seconds.

But the matters were made worse because the next track in line started with a very quiet, very long intro. Because of how quiet we ran our pre-service music and how loud the congregation was in greeting each other, it sounded like complete silence. For 20 seconds.

You could actually hear the room start to quiet down because the silence distracted them. They were wondering what was going on.

"Am I supposed to be quiet now? Is the service starting?" And the next 20 seconds would be the congregation staring at the band on stage and the band staring awkwardly back. They didn't want to jump the 20 seconds left on the visual countdown, so they just had to wait in silence until it was time to play.

Again, this happened far too often. I eventually learned to program a track into the video countdown that ended perfectly when the clock struck zero. Or when that wasn't an option I made sure the tracks in the pre-service music loop blended seamlessly and there were no awkward gaps of silence.

After the Service
Another source of frustration for me came when our sound team, worship team and pastor hadn't communicated the plan for the end of the service. Standard protocol was to kick off our pre-service mix as soon as the service ended so the energy in the room would pump right back up. (Mind you, the track with a silent opening happened a few times post-service too.)

But on some Sundays, our pastor wanted to end the service in a time of prayer. Either our sound team wasn't paying attention or our worship team wasn't. Sometimes the pastor wanted a moment of silent keyboard playing and the sound team kicked off the loud music anyway. Or sometimes the worship leader missed the memo and stopped playing, while the sound team *had* received the memo and didn't play the loud music. That meant silence and an awkward time for everyone involved—especially when the pastor snapped at the worship leader with his microphone still on.

Avoid this awkwardness by communicating and planning ahead. Let each party know what their role will be as the service starts and as it ends. Communicate clearly and often. These moments are the first and last things your guests will remember about the service. Make them clean and flawless.

Chapter 35

The Absent Pastor

I know of some churches that let their pastor vacation the whole summer. Their motives are great. They want to help keep their pastor from getting burnt out from speaking and having to prepare sermons each week. I respect the heart behind this philosophy.

Unfortunately, I visited one of those churches during the summer, while trying to find a new church home. Each week, I drove to the church expecting to hear the pastor. But he never spoke. It was a long sequence of guest speakers.

Their messages were great. They pulled out their A-level material for these Sundays. But I never got a chance to hear from the leader of the church. I never got a chance to hear the heart behind the person I'd submit my life to spiritually. I never got a chance to trust the guy because I never heard from him.

I came to the church for four weeks but eventually gave up. I went to another church whose pastor I immediately connected with. I immediately heard his heart, and then the second week confirmed it. I knew this was a guy I'd be happy to learn from and become like.

It's tempting for church workers to diminish the

Unwelcome

role of the pastor in a church. We'd like to think it's the sum of all the parts that make a church what it is. We'd hope the worship has an equal impact as the message. The ministries have equal impact as the church service. But it doesn't work like that. The pastor is the heart and core of the church.

In Luke 6:40, Jesus tells his disciples that a student, once fully trained, will be just like their teacher. The pastor, the teaching team—however you approach ministry at your church—is the teacher of the church. They set the standard their students (the congregation) will eventually follow.

While your guests might not be able to verbalize this, they feel it. We look to our pastors as a big part of our life. We want to make sure we (1) like the pastor(s), (2) trust them and (3) want to hear their voice each week for an entire sermon.

I understand the need for guest speakers. A pastor needs a break. But I recommend you limit the consecutive weeks you allow guest speakers to dominate the pulpit.

Some churches record their pastor via video ahead of time when the pastor will be out of town for many weeks. This allows them to play the videos on the weekends they're gone. It gives guests the consistency of the pastor even during vacation.

Some churches are satisfied having a family member speak. Pastors' kids, while they may approach ministry differently than their parent, carry so much of the heart of their parents. They make a great guest speaker that can still give guests a glimpse into the pastor's heart. People saw me (a pastor's son) as an extension of my father. They gave me much more liberty to speak into their life—even though the only extra authority I had was my father's genes.

Finally, a teaching team or associate pastor does a great job at translating the heart of the pastor. It's still not the same as the pastor, but guests know there will be a lot of heart overlap because they work so closely together.

Many churches, when they are forced to have a guest speaker deliver the message on a Sunday, are great about informing the congregation when the pastor will be back in the pulpit. That's a great way to let first-time guests know exactly what they can expect.

Each week, do your best to present the true you to the guests who grace your doors. When you show them who you are, it gives them the liberty to stay because they know you're the right fit. Or it gives them the liberty to find the church that's right for them. Let's love our guests and make this decision as easy as possible for them.

Chapter 36

The Cultural Reference

YOLO—you only live once—used to be the motto of the young and the reckless. Now it's the motto of desperate parents trying to relate to their teens—and failing.

Only two months after Drake released the song where he coined the phrase, people were already sick of it. And a few years later, some people are just now figuring out what it means and then incorporating it into their services in an attempt at relevance. Unfortunately, it's too little too late.

When you try to take part in a cultural phenomenon after its prime, you simply look irrelevant to outsiders and guests. And modern culture is moving fast! Within a few months the Harlem Shake overtook the Internet. Then it went dead just as fast as it entered the world. It's really easy to get lost in the dust of culture and feel like you're behind.

So what's the solution? Do you tirelessly pursue culture and make sure you're abreast of the latest trends?

That's one solution. You might want to grab some teens or college students and bring them into your planning meetings. Be sure you aren't totally missing cultural context by allowing the

Unwelcome

younger generations to speak into your planning.

But there's a better solution. Don't try so hard to copy pop culture. Don't be so worried about "relating" to this generation you forget what *really* relates to people.

As a parent, you'll never be able to relate with your teen like you're one of their peers. Teens make it that way on purpose. As soon as adults catch on to a bit of culture popular to teenagers, they change it. As soon as parents are doing something, it's no longer cool. But if the parent really wants to relate to their kid, they'll love them. They'll be honest with them. They'll listen to them.

There's absolutely nothing wrong with being culturally relevant. Just like a missionary learns a culture's language when they want to minister to them, it's wise for us to speak our culture's language. Keep your ears and eyes open. Observe what's going on around you.

But don't assume the only way to reach a culture is to reference all their favorite TV shows and rap songs. You can reach them without that. We have the most relevant message and story on earth. It's relevant to people because it's what they need. You don't have to try to package it so much. It's truth. And truth is relevant.

Chapter 37

The Simple Menu

Have you ever had the chance to visit In-n-Out Burger? It's a Christian-owned business that started in California and is slowly spreading all over the nation.

The first time I visited the burger joint, I was impressed with their menu. It had four items: burgers, fries, drinks and shakes. Sure, you could get cheese on your burger or multiple patties, but there wasn't much more to it. It was so refreshing.

I'd never been to the restaurant before. So normally it would have taken me 10 minutes to read through all the items and make my decision. But I instantly knew what I wanted based on how hungry I was, and I got my food fast. It was an amazing experience.

As I visited the restaurant more and learned more about it, I soon discovered their secret menu. You could order things different ways and get things newcomers didn't know about. But I never ceased to appreciate the simplicity of their menu.

A guest in your church doesn't need to be bombarded with 30 different ministries they should get involved with during the week. They don't need the pressure. And if you're making an announcement to the congregation from the

Unwelcome

pulpit, you're pressuring them to get involved with what you're announcing.

So many times our services—at least the announcement portion—can seem like a bloated menu at a restaurant. And not only do we list everything we offer, we give long-winded explanations of what each one's about. We give funny stories or design special logos for each menu item. We think the more menu items we have, the better it looks to a newcomer.

But really, it can overwhelm the guest and leave them wishing they went to a different restaurant.

There's a show I like to watch where an expert helps failing restaurants save their business. One of the things I always notice he does is reduce long menus to only a few items. He makes sure each of those items is of supreme quality and leaves it at that. If the menu fits on one page, his job is done.

Imagine if we gave ourselves only one or two minutes to make announcements. You'd limit what you said and make sure every single item you announced was completely relevant to the entire congregation. You could refer people to the bulletin or the website to get full details on everything you offered. But you'd focus your two minutes on what applied to everyone.

Can it be done? You bet it can. And it's a wonderfully refreshing thing for guests. They know exactly what their next step is, and their decision-making process is so much easier.

Chapter 38

The Weird Class

I remember inviting a friend to attend church with me. I invited him to the church where I worked. He loved the service! He decided he'd definitely come back and get very involved.

The next week, I saw him during the service, and he looked a little bewildered.

"What's up?" I asked.

He replied, "I wanted to get involved in a Sunday school class I saw offered in the bulletin. I showed up, and it was just one family and me. And the family was very awkward. They tried to make me feel welcomed, but it was a very uncomfortable hour. And I'm pretty sure there was a little heresy in that class."

Fortunately, my friend had already bought into the church. He knew he'd make this church his home. But he felt a little betrayed we suggested he attend this Sunday school class that was progressing very unsuccessfully.

The back-story to the Sunday school class is that a long-time member wanted to start a class. We knew he was a bit weird and didn't quite believe the same things as our church. But we figured it wouldn't hurt anything.

Unfortunately, to be fair to every Sunday school class, we promoted them all equally. So his poorly performing Sunday school class was right alongside our most successful one.

The same number of newcomers visited his class (and were promptly scared away) as visited the successful class. Does that seem fair? Perhaps it's fair to the Sunday school teacher. But it's very unfair to the guests who trusted we wouldn't send them somewhere we didn't highly endorse.

Any time something makes it to your bulletin or gets promoted from the pulpit, you're putting your church's full seal of approval on it. Proverbs 22:1 says, "A good name is more desirable than great riches." And when we lose our credibility as a church, we lose our great name. What a costly mistake!

If you want to keep a good name, or restore your church's good name, it'll probably require some changes. Either you'll need to change the way you promote your ministries/events, or you might need to make the tough decision to discontinue certain things.

You might avoid promoting each Sunday school class equally. You might instead have guests and newcomers sign an interest form, then you assign them to a Sunday school class.

Or, better, you might encourage the leaders of these unsuccessful groups to get involved with a successful group. You might encourage them to assist or take part in a way that still shows they're valued, but doesn't give them full control.

When guests attend an event you endorse, they're placing their trust in your hands. Treat that trust with so much care. How you treat their trust is how you show you love and care for your guests.

Communication

Chapter 39

The Hype

- "We're so happy you visited us at church!"
- "Join us for this life-changing worship night!"
- "Your life will never be the same if you attend this small group!"
- "This Bible verse will blow your mind!"
- "This missionary's talk will show you how to make all your wildest dreams come true!"
- "God will give you millions of dollars if you start tithing!"

OK, so maybe some of those got a bit out of hand. But have you ever noticed how quickly we throw phrases like "life changing" around? If my life had actually changed with every "life-changing" event I've attended, I'm pretty sure I wouldn't even recognize myself.

I've found, in church communication, we throw around hyperboles and exclamation points the most when we don't quite know how to market something.

For instance, we have a women's event coming up, and rather than learn more about the event and why a woman might want to attend, we just throw around bold statements and exclamation points. A woman can make some lasting friendships and connections at the end, but instead we say their lives will forever be changed. They could get inspired and encouraged at the event, but we tell them it'll forever change the way they see womanhood.

We can't promise those things. So we shouldn't promote them like that.

People in our church communities are used to being marketed to each week. They live in the real world, and they see thousands of advertisements weekly. Each ad is promising them success, fame, sex and love. And each ad falls short in delivery. Why would we want to lump our church communications in with those things?

We don't need to market to our church communities. We need to minister to them. We need to speak truth to them. Whisper possibilities instead of yelling hyperboles. Be honest about what they can expect instead of trying to compete with the other ads they'll see.

If you consistently create great experiences for people, you'll never have to use a single exclamation point to market them. Your own people will use plenty of exclamation points themselves. They'll spread the word to their friends and family for you. They'll talk you up, so you don't have to. And you'll give people a break from the marketing messages. You won't join the noise of people trying to sell them something.

Chapter 40

The Over-Stuffed Bulletin

Do you remember those prank peanut cans? You'd buy one at a novelty store, and then give it to one of your friends. "Want some peanuts?" They'd say, "Sure!" But once they opened the can, a fake snake exploded out of the can and flew toward their face.

Maybe I'm remembering it more dramatically than it was, but there were a few Sundays where our church bulletin felt like a prank peanut can. There were so many inserts and announcements in the bulletin that it felt like a ticker-tape parade in the lobby. So many flyers shot out of the overstuffed bulletin that there were papers falling all over as the greeters handed them out.

The chairs inside the sanctuary looked pretty much the same. It was obvious each of our guests and attendees had big bulletin mishaps and didn't think it was worth picking them up.

Besides the fact that it was a huge waste of paper and even more money, we should have been more intentional with what we were advertising to our people. Our theory was it would be easier to let each ministry advertise whatever they wanted. It would be less drama and less work on the part of the communications team. But instead, we just made a mess.

Unwelcome

When my family and I were missionaries in Guatemala, we used to take short-term missions teams around the country to show them the sights and sounds. The last day of their trip, we'd always take our guests to a typical market. It was in the town square of a nearby village. There you could buy all the brightly colored bracelets and hacky sacks you could fit into your luggage.

My family was very used to the scenario, but our tourist friends weren't prepared for it. It was always fun to watch them walk through the market. They'd get so overwhelmed. Each vendor poked their head out of their kiosk and in broken English said, "Come over here. Buy from me. I have high quality. Hacky sacks for only five quetzales (Guatemalan currency)."

Every single vendor tried to put the squeeze on these potential buyers. They each used salesmanship and emotional manipulation to get them to buy their homemade goods. Talk about pressure!

I don't think churches' overstuffed bulletins are much different than this. Our regular attendees are used to all the pressure falling out of their bulletin. But the first-time guests are overwhelmed. Each falling paper is pressuring them to attend an event or give to a project. It's too much.

Imagine if we loved our guests enough to make things simple for them. What if we curated our announcements? What if we chose the one or two things we wanted to communicate or advertise to guests and kept it to that? Do you think we'd be more effective? Do you think you'd get a bigger response by advertising just one event instead of 10?

I guarantee you would. And your guests wouldn't have to feel the pressure.

Chapter 41

The Out-Dated Online Info

I don't think there's a single church in the world that intentionally puts incorrect information on the Internet.

Unfortunately, it happens. You change your service times—either permanently or for a single event—and you forget to update the website. Or you update the website, but you forget one page on the site and neglect to update the information there.

So Sunday morning rolls around, and a guest shows up an hour before the service starts. Or they show up 10 minutes before it ends. And they feel stupid. Did they remember the service time wrong? They check the site. They feel betrayed. They just missed the service.

They already had enough fear and anxiety over going to a new place to worship. They'd already overcome many obstacles that sought to prevent them from getting to the church—traffic, crying children and construction. So they leave feeling dejected and discouraged.

I don't care if the little bit of the service they experienced was phenomenal. There's a good chance they won't come back.

Unwelcome

It's so important we give our first-time guests accurate information. That means a few things:

- **Update the site early.** If you update your website on the Friday of the week you're changing the service times, you're doing it too late. You should update the site as soon as the last service at that old time is over.
- **Check every page on your site.** The incorrect service times might be buried within the site. Did you check the "what to expect" page? Did you check the "contact us" page? Did you get the time on the front page? On the footer? Scour the site and even get a friend to check it too.
- **Check all your social media profiles.** Does Facebook have the correct service times? Twitter? Instagram? If you put the information out there, you need to make sure it's accurate.

Your website is a guest's first impression of your church. It's a chance to answer questions and address concerns before Sunday morning. And the answers you post on your website (like service times) are your first promises to first-time guests. Don't break those promises. When you establish honesty early on, it sets the tone for the rest of your relationship with that guest. Make sure that tone is a good one.

Chapter 42

The Wrong Location

One Sunday a guest showed up 30 minutes before our service began. They were obviously very confused. The guest approached me. "I thought your services began at 9:30 a.m.?"

I replied, "No sir. Our two service times are 10 a.m. and 11:30 a.m."

"That's not what the website said."

Now, I'm the one who managed the website. So I knew precisely what it said. I'd verified every single page on the site had accurate service times. So I asked him, "Would you be able to show me where you saw that?"

He googled our church name, Summit Church. He pulled up the first site and said, "There it is—9:30 a.m. and 11 a.m."

It wasn't our church. It was a Summit Church in another state. Unfortunately, you wouldn't have known the church was in another state until you dug multiple depths into the website's navigation structure.

While this unfortunate occurrence was completely outside of my control, it re-affirmed something I believe in strongly. A church shouldn't make you guess where it's located. Unless you're the only Summit Church or First Baptist Church in the whole world, you should make it excessively clear where you're located—state, city and even street. If the only place on your site that says your location is the "Contact Us" page or the "Get Directions" page, you're going to miss many people.

We'd like to assume everyone reads our URL on the church sign or they all come to our site the same way. But people won't remember URLs—even simple ones. And people arrive at your site through Google, Twitter and even misspelled/misremembered URLs.

Be excessively clear about where your church is located. It's a bigger part of your brand than your sermon series or a picture of your pastor.

Chapter 43

The Website Photos

Stock photos are a wonderful resource. They allow you to plaster beautiful faces anywhere you need them. You want a nice looking Filipino man holding a cell phone? There's a stock photo for that. You want a girl at the beach doing a cartwheel? There's a stock photo for that too.

And if you want an ethnically diverse group of people for your website to show your church embraces diversity, there's most definitely a stock photo for that. Unfortunately, if that stock photo doesn't actually represent your church, you're lying to your website visitors.

One of the main reasons newcomers visit a church website is to see what the church is like. "What types of people go there? Will there be someone like me there? Are there people my age at the church? Do people from my socio-economic strata attend?"

The danger of using stock photos is that it's tempting to show you reach everyone. So you grab a white child, a black man, a Hispanic grandma and an Asian American college student and put them all in one photo.

But what if your church is primarily filled with Hispanic grandmas? You lied about the other

Unwelcome

three people. A young black man will visit your church and say, "What happened? Where are all the other people like me?"

I'm not saying you shouldn't use stock photos on your website. I'm not even saying you should stop using diversity in your photos. But the majority of the photos you use on your website should represent people who actually attend your church.

If your church is primarily filled with affluent white families, there's a reason for that. That means they're the primary type of person you reach. It doesn't mean you won't reach other people. It doesn't mean you don't want to reach other types of people. But for whatever reason— the style of worship or the personality of the pastor—you reach mostly affluent white families.

That's OK. Different types of churches appeal to different types of people. I believe diversity within the church is important. But if you're advertising age and ethnic diversity and only have white grandparents in your church, you're lying to people.

Let your guests see what your church is like before they even set foot in your building. Give them a sample of the types of people they'll see. Let them see there are people like them who attend. Show them love by showing your people.

Chapter 44

The Forgotten Social Media Account

When I worked as the communications director at my church, I was tempted to put our church everywhere. If there was a new social media platform, I went there. I made profiles for our church on Facebook, Twitter, Instagram, Myspace, Quora... If there was a social media option, I was there.

I even made multiple accounts sometimes. Our youth had an account. Our college ministry. Our worship ministry. You could say I went profile happy.

Unfortunately, I completely lacked the capacity to remember all the accounts I created—much less monitor them. Consequently, I'd run into an email every now and then that said, "I tried to contact you via [insert social media name here] and didn't get a response. I was wondering..."

When I checked the profile, I realized they weren't the only ones asking questions there. Multiple folks had reached out, wanting to visit our church or get other information. And I'd failed them. I'd completely ignored them. You can bet I felt like a big old jerk.

It can be tempting to jump on the bandwagon of every new social media tool. Each time a new

Unwelcome

entity enters the scene, there are multiple social media gurus touting it as the next big thing. "Your organization needs to be here. If you hope to make an impact on your community, this is a must for you."

So you hop on the site, create a profile, engage with it for a week or two, and then forget about it when no one's responding on it. But you also forget to delete the account. Then as that social media entity grows and gains more users, people start engaging. And you've already stopped listening.

I encourage you to keep an accurate list of every social media profile you create. Delete the ones you no longer want. Then create systems for monitoring and actively updating the social media profiles. Create reminders, tasks, calendar events, etc.

There's nothing wrong with jumping on every social media bandwagon as long as you're able to maintain the communication. If you find you aren't able to maintain communication, choose very selectively which accounts you'll keep. Analyze your congregation and the types of people you want to reach. Then get on the social media outlets they actually use.

Accurate communication on a few key social media outlets beats out slow and unresponsive profiles all across the web.

If you create a touch point with people, they'll reach out. Make sure you're ready and able to respond when they do.

Chapter 45

The Unwanted Volunteer

My wife and I had just moved to a new city. We immediately found the church we wanted to attend and get plugged into. So the same night after our first visit to the church, I got on their website and signed up to volunteer. I emailed a couple of people and said, "I'd love to volunteer." I reached out.

Oddly enough, I didn't get a single email response that week. So after church the next Sunday, I went to the guest services area. We got the full schpeel about the church and that volunteering was the best way to get involved. I took the opportunity to let the guest service attendant know we wanted to volunteer. "Where do we sign up?"

He actually seemed a bit surprised I was so eager. But he found a volunteer coordinator and referred us to them. We repeated the same request. "We want to get involved."

Finally, he told us he'd let the respective ministry heads know we were eager to volunteer, and they'd be in contact with us.

Do I need to tell what happened—or rather what didn't? We never heard anything from anyone. Neither my wife nor me.

It wasn't until we stuck around for a little while that we realized their funnel for getting people involved in serving was through their membership class. And they held this membership class only once a quarter.

We felt unneeded and unwanted.

We tried the church for a while, but we wanted to get involved. And we felt this church (1) didn't really need our contribution and (2) would take a long time to let us serve. So we started going to a church where we felt like we were needed.

So many times our churches desperately want people to get involved. But we don't have a system in place to actually grab people who show interest.

It's sort of like the dog chasing cars. One day he finally caught one. "Now what do I do with this thing?"

Do you have a system set up to quickly respond to guests and congregation members who want to get involved? Do you know what to do with a volunteer when you catch one?

If a guest wants to attend a small group, can they get in one quickly? Or do they have to wait until the next season when the small groups start over?

If a guest wants to start serving, is there a swift system in place to get them from point A to point B? Or do they have to attend multiple weeks of classes before they can get involved?

If a guest asks a question from an unexpected place—like an email or a tweet—is there someone who will catch those questions? Or do you require all prayer requests to come from a card in the seats or an online form?

A church that responds quickly to people is a church that loves people. But sometimes our systems can get in the way of that. Make sure your systems are efficient and there's plenty of overlap. Make sure no question or sign of interest falls through the cracks. Respond quickly, and make it easy for guests when they want to get involved or get more information.

Chapter 46

The Biblically Illiterate Guest

I was in town visiting some family, and I went to a very large church in the area. Part of their success came from the fact they never talked down to people. They never made a guest feel bad for being new to the Bible or new to Christianity. Because of that, they drew a huge number of new believers and non-Christians. The church was massively successful at outreach and evangelism. I love this particular church.

The Sunday I visited, though, they'd invited a well-known guest speaker to address their congregation. I'd heard good things about this guy, so I was excited to hear from him.

I was rather disappointed, though. He had great things to say, but he continually talked down to the congregation. At times he even lambasted them for not knowing the Bible enough.

He said, "Now, we all know the story of Job. Right? ... You do know the story of Job... Please tell me you know the story of Job. I can't believe you don't know enough about the Bible to know about Job..."

With each new sentence it got more and more uncomfortable. He was ridiculing these new believers who had put their trust in this church.

Unwelcome

He was dismantling the good reputation of this church. He was breaking their trust.

Now, I know the story of Job. I understand and wish our nation's biblical literary weren't so low. But criticizing and belittling people won't make them more eager to crack open their Bibles. It'll make them think you're a jerk and stop listening.

We can't afford to do this if we hope to embrace guests and new believers in our churches.

We don't need to water down the Bible, but we also can't assume everyone in our room fully understands what we're talking about.

So what's the solution? How do we find an appropriate balance?

It's the same thing you'd do if you invited guests over to a family dinner. You give them context. You explain stories. You introduce people to the "characters" in your family. You don't assume they know everything.

You don't have to keep the conversation shallow when you invite people over to your house. But you slow it down a little bit to make sure they're on board with what people are saying.

This is exactly what we can do in our churches. Bring them along on the journey. Guests—even biblically literate guests—will be so grateful you include them in the narrative, that you give them context and welcome them into the conversation.

Chapter 47

The Long-Winded Pastor

I used to work closely with a pastor at my church who oversaw the ministry to young adults and college students. His title was the young adults pastor, so I affectionately referred to him as the YAP (he didn't like that so much).

But he was a bit of a yap. He easily spoke longer than an hour in a service that was only meant to be an hour and 15 minutes long (we advertised this on all our signage). He was aware he frequently went over the allotted time, but he didn't really care.

And one of the things he'd always ask as he was passing the hour-and-15-minute mark is, "You guys don't mind if the message goes a little bit longer, right?"

Well, one evening I got the guts to say, "Yes, we mind."

Now, I understand that was massively disrespectful. I was a teenage punk. I fully embrace that I was in the wrong. But my rhetoric was sound.

I wanted to shock him into realizing nobody will ever say, "No, please don't go longer." If someone actually said that in response to a preacher, they'd sound both disrespectful and unspiritual. Right? So who would willingly put themselves in that position?

I took one for the team.

I apologized later. And we mended the relationship. And he got the point. So I still think it might have been worth it.

People's time is valuable. I'm not saying your sermons have to be short. But you should decide how long the service will go ahead of time, and make sure you stick with that.

One of the things I've found that eats away so much at a pastor's time to preach is the announcements, offering and other transitional elements. The crazy thing about it all is those are toward the beginning of the service. Thus, if they run long, it leaves the pastor with less time to deliver the message.

What if you were more structured in your announcement time? What if you only allotted two minutes for announcements or 10 minutes for offering *and* announcements? By controlling the timing in the less important portions of the service, you'll make sure you have time for the parts that really matter. Then you won't be left asking for more time when the service should be ending.

Respect your congregation's time. Respect your guests' time. Remember what it says in Ephesians 5:16: "Redeeming the time, because the days are evil." Redeem your service time, and redeem your guests for a second visit.

The Big Picture

Chapter 48

The Weird Stuff

I love watching baptisms. It's so exciting to see people make a public declaration of their faith by symbolically being buried with Christ and resurrected to new life. It's an event worth celebrating.

Have you ever thought about how weird a baptism would be, though, if you didn't know what was going on? Imagine watching a video of a baptism without audio. Most baptisms might look a bit like a murderer trying to drown a victim. The pastor shoves a guy under water, then the "victim" bursts back out gasping for air. Then everyone claps.

Looks a bit weird, huh? I think if we were honest, we'd admit churches tend to do a lot of weird stuff. I'm not talking about snake handling or chanting Latin phrases (though that's some bizarre behavior that could freak out a first-time guest). I'm talking about the regular things churches do all the time. We do stuff nobody else does and we need to realize how weird it can be for someone who's new to church.

- We fund our activities by passing around a metal plate, asking people to drop in their money. That might work for a group of friends buying a pizza, but that's not how most nonprofit organizations do it.

- At the end of our services we call people forward to get a deeper experience. In an era of clergy sexual abuse cases, we're laying hands on people and they're getting weepy.
- Some churches have the entire congregation speaking in unison.
- Then we have a solemn ceremony each month where we eat bread we refer to as flesh and drink wine (or grape juice) we call blood. What is this, zombies versus vampires?

Between offerings and altar calls, liturgy and communion, churches do some weird stuff. We see it all the time and it's become normal, but to a visitor it can look a bit spooky.

Now, I'm not criticizing these church practices. I believe wholeheartedly in their validity and take part myself. There's nothing wrong with passing around a metal plate or a basket to receive an offering. And there's everything right with receiving the Lord's supper.

But it's important we acknowledge how weird these things can seem to outsiders and first-time guests. In Western culture, church has become a place not just for believers, but for unbelievers who are curious as well. Sometimes church is even for atheists who are merely fulfilling a family tradition by attending on Easter and Christmas.

So it's not a matter of whether or not you'll have outsiders in your congregation, but when and how often. More than that, it's an issue of whether or not they'll be scared away or feel welcomed to come back.

A few weeks ago I visited a CrossFit class. If you're unfamiliar with CrossFit, it's an international fitness program that uses a mixture of gymnastics, weight lifting and physical torture to whip you into shape (maybe I exaggerated on that last part).

My wife had been begging me for months to attend a class with her. I finally relented and agreed to go. I was nervous. I knew I'd be an obvious newcomer, surrounded by girls wearing lululemon and guys with large neck muscles. I'd stick out like a sore thumb. Come to think of it, my thumb was sore after the workout.

The class could have easily intimidated me. They had us swing kettlebells, flail around on the floor and attach thick rubber bands to bars to help us do pull-ups. This stuff all seemed a little foreign to me. It was a bit weird. I was intimidated.

It reminded me of what newcomers must experience at church.

Fortunately, my coach was aware that these things might seem weird to me. He was quick to explain and even sit next to me and coach me as I performed the movements. He made sure I knew where I could get water, where I could find the apparatuses and kept me from trying to lift too much weight. I felt safe, even though everything around me seemed scary and made me want to run away.

That was the key. That's what encouraged me to come back. My next time was even more stuff I didn't understand. But the coach again talked me through it.

That's the key for your church. Yes, there will be weird stuff newcomers won't understand. Yes, they'll even get a bit scared. But when we love our guests enough to walk them through it all, it makes them feel safe. It gives them an opportunity to learn and to even ask questions.

So how do we practically do this in our churches? Sometimes it might be as simple as printed instructions in the bulletin. It might be taking advantage of projection screens to offer some explanation. You might talk through it from the stage or prepare your ushers to explain things as they're seating people.

There are many ways you can help guests overcome the "weirdness" in your church service. The key is to make it a priority. Look for every opportunity to explain. Don't assume your guests know everything that's happening.

That's the difference between a guest clapping after a baptism, or bum rushing the baptismal trying to save a drowning man from a murdering pastor. OK, that doesn't happen. But your guest shouldn't have to figure out what's going on. Don't let your guests feel lost and confused when you're the one doing something weird.

Chapter 49

The Perfectly Imperfect

My niece recently asked my sister—her mom—where babies come from. My sister isn't the type to sugarcoat or answer in fairytale-speak. But without getting too detailed about the reproductive process—so she wouldn't traumatize her three year-old—she explained it in somewhat vague terms. When I asked my niece what my sister told her, she said this:

A little thing that looks like a fish swims into a ball. When the fish gets inside, its tail falls off. The one goo mixes with the other goo and then a baby is formed!

While that explanation was perfectly acceptable for my little niece, the description traumatized me. What a messy business!

But that's also a pretty good description of how life happens. It's messy! And it's frankly a bit confusing how it works.

That's life!

Sometimes, in our attempt to build a thriving church that creates an amazing experience for our first-time guests, we over-program. We focus too much on perfection. We have all our ducks in a row, and we leave no room for mess.

Unwelcome

Consequently, we take life out of the equation. In our attempt to keep things clean and perfect, we lose the goo that creates life. We forget about love. We forget about grace. We forget about heart. It's important we don't lose the life in our churches.

I've been to churches that do everything right. They have the perfect parking team, the flawless band, the silly video illustrations and the gifted speaker. They never go longer than the allotted time for each service. Their graphics are fantastic. Yet I leave their service feeling no life. There's no heart.

Then I've been to services that make mistakes. Their musicians aren't the best. There are flaws in their parking or kids programs. And those churches are bursting at the seams because people love being around life. They invite their friends. Then those friends invite *their* friends. Life attracts life.

Strive for quality. Work out the kinks in your service and in the first impressions people receive from your church. But don't strangle the life out of the church. Manage what you can, but let life happen.

Chapter 50

The Why

"I want to do a sermon series on the context of the Bible," my dad told us in our creative team meeting. "I want to put the major events of the Bible in historical order and provide context for those stories so our congregation can better understand the book when they read it."

Lame. I wasn't excited about this sermon idea. I thought it would be boring. But I set to work to come up with any idea that would salvage this dreadful sermon series.

One morning in the shower it hit me: Monty Python and Mel Brooks. What if we named this series "The History of the World"? What if we turned it into a mixture of comedy sketches and information?

This idea was brilliant. It salvaged a boring set of Sundays and turned it into something I was excited about. "The History of the World: A somewhat theatrical, somewhat comedic series in three parts."

For each segment of the Bible (about 12 each Sunday), we created mini comedic sketches. Some were direct rip-offs of Monty Python sketches, some were based on terribly bad wordplay and still others were just completely random.

Unwelcome

We had the congregation throw confetti eggs at the actors to illustrate the period of Exile. (Eggs aisle... See? Terribly bad wordplay.) We served our actors rich, chocolaty Constantine (Ovaltine) to illustrate the rule of Constantine. And for some reason we even put our quasi-British host into a coma and set him on fire.

It was probably the most memorable series we'd ever done. We had laughs like we'd never experienced before. People still talk about the event today. But when I look back on the series, I realize now it was a complete failure.

First of all, nobody remembered any of the content from the sermon series. They don't remember any context on the Bible—the "creativity" completely overshadowed the information from the series.

Secondly, I realize we did this sermon series because we were bored with church. We forgot the "why" behind what we were doing.

Anytime you forget why you're doing what you're doing, you run the risk of making a mistake like this. If you find yourself just going through the motions of church and becoming bored with the event, you'll look for ways to jazz it up. You'll look for ways to turn a life-changing event into an entertaining event.

It's so important we remember why we gather in our churches. It isn't just a weekly tradition we do to make God happy with us. Our Sunday (or Saturday or Wednesday) gatherings have real purpose.

Our job as ministers and pastors is to "equip the saints for the work of ministry" (Ephesians 4:12). How can we do that if we're looking for ways to simply keep church from being boring?

What we do in our church services matters. It doesn't mean we can't have fun. It doesn't mean it won't be occasionally entertaining for people who attend. But we must remember why we do what we do. It matters. And your guests know it matters.

Appendix

I think we all have a friend who doesn't exactly have the freshest armpits on a daily basis. In our group of friends, we can all smell the stink, but he just doesn't seem to realize. And nobody feels comfortable enough telling this friend he needs some deodorant. So the stink just persists, day in and day out.

We all have blind spots in our lives—areas where we're unaware our armpits stink. Everyone else can smell them, but nobody wants to tell you. And they often keep people from hanging around with us.

Churches are no different. Churches have stinky pits too.

So how do you find out you smell stinky? And how do you find out how to fix the problem? You ask. You ask someone to be honest enough to point out the areas where you need to improve.

Businesses do this all the time. They call these friends secret shoppers. A secret shopper merely visits the store or business, goes through the motions a normal customer would go through, and then reports back on what they noticed. This feedback from secret shoppers is invaluable because it helps the business see what a typical

Unwelcome

customer sees, which the business might not see.

Your church can do this too. You can get secret shoppers to visit your service and report back to you. And it isn't a complicated process.

Often, people are very willing to help if you merely ask. Or you could put out an ad on Craigslist and offer a gift card in return. Or find a friend of a friend.

Regardless of where you find your secret shopper, I highly recommend every church go through this process.

To make it easier, this book has a couple questions you can use to interview your secret shopper after the visit. Why not put these questions on a form and send them in with the secret shopper?

Then your church team can use the responses to make informed decisions about things that might need to change in your service. You don't need to change every single thing they mention or dislike. But chances are, some things they respond with will resonate inside the team. Your eyes will open to the areas where your pits are stinky. Then all you need to do is make those changes.

So try out these questions, and see how your secret shoppers respond. You might be surprised.

Some Questions to Ask Your Secret Shopper

If you had to describe our service to a friend, how would you explain it?

Do you know where the bathrooms are located?

Did our child check-in process go smoothly?

Did we use any words/terms during the service you weren't familiar with?

How would you rate the following factors of our service?
(1-Very Poor, 2-Poor, 3-Mediocre, 4-Good, 5-Very Good)

1. Ease of finding a parking spot.
2. Friendliness of the parking attendants.
3. Ease of finding the entrance to the service.
4. Friendliness/helpfulness of greeters or ushers.
5. Cleanliness of the facilities.
6. Friendliness of congregation.

If you marked any of these as a Poor or Very Poor, would you mind explaining what we did wrong, and how we could improve?

What was your impression of the worship team?

What was your impression of the pastor?

Did you leave the service excited to return next week?

What did we do *really* well in our services (if anything)?

What could we improve on?

Jonathan Malm is a creative entrepreneur and writer. He's the author of *Created for More*. He also runs Sunday| Magazine and Church Stage Design Ideas. You can follow Jonathan online at JonathanMalm.com or on Twitter @JonathanMalm.

Created for More: 30 Days to Seeing Your World in a New Way

This 30-day devotional is intended for creatives—writers, artists, photographers, videographers, problem solvers—both within and outside the church, to help them see the world differently and get out of a creative rut. This little gem of a book belongs on the shelf of every church creative.

Unwelcome

We are a firebrand of communicators, sparking churches to communicate the gospel clearly, effectively and without compromise.

We are made up of passionate change agents, experienced communication professionals and thoughtful instigators; advocating for communicators to find their place in the church—and helping the church get through to their communities so that churches know who they are and are unashamed to tell others.

We identify, resource and celebrate the next generation of church communicators, encouraging them to focus their tenacity and talent for excellent communication, so that churches are sought out by the communities they serve.

We provide smart coaching and mentoring through social media, publishing, events and one-on-one relationships, spotlighting communication that is true, good and beautiful—prompting others to do the same—so that more outsiders become a part of a church community.

We remove barriers to change the way people see Christians and how they speak about the church by promoting relationships, resources, ideas

Unwelcome

and models for communication. We collaborate people's gifts/skills to work in concert with the Creator and their local church.

As God's story comes alive to us and others, we see gospel-centered local churches that captivate the attention and liberate the imagination of their community, resulting in more people saying, **"That's what church should be!"**

Center for Church Communication:
Courageous storytellers welcome.

Visit CFCCLabs.org to learn more about our projects and get involved.

For more practical tips, inspiration and stories from fellow communicators, visit our flagship blog, ChurchMarketingSucks.com.

The Getting Started Series

Making your first-time guests feel welcome is a big step. It's an important part of how your church communicates. To keep improving how you communicate, we've created a series of introductory resources:

Getting Started in Church Communication: Web Basics

If your church needs a website or a better one, this is the place to start. Timeless strategy, practical details and realistic expectations are the order of the day, rather than specific techie details that will be outdated next week. 15 chapters cover a range of web topics, including first impressions, the call to action, designing for mobile and more.

Here's to church websites that wow.

Getting Started in Church Communication: Copy Matters

Writing is a foundational communication skill and your church needs to wield words with wonder. You'll find practical writing tips and techniques, plus specific ideas to improve your copy and fine-tune your writing process. 14 chapters cover a range of writing issues, including writing for email, social media and heathens, as well as style guides and proofreading.

The written word needs to be written well.

Getting Started in Church Communication: Landing a Job

Landing that first job—or a new one—is a significant hurdle and it's OK to get help. This detailed road map will walk you through the job process, from internships to interviews, portfolios to prayer. 14 chapters help you get hired, including practical tips on networking, how to prepare yourself, what churches are looking for and more.

Your new job is waiting.

Visit GettingStartedSeries.com to learn more about these books.

Unwelcome

Acknowledgments

This book is a result of many people's hard work. I got to write it, but it wouldn't have happened without the following people:

My dad, Rick Malm, for helping me edit this book and providing his insights as a pastor.

Every church that does these things right. It's always so exciting to walk into a new church and feel a wave of welcome wash over you.

Josh White for encouraging me that this book needed to be made.

Chuck Scoggins for working with me to get the Center for Church Communications team on board with the project.

Kevin D. Hendricks for editing and brainstorming with us ad nauseum on the project. A special editing shout out also goes to Elizabyth Ladwig.

Katie Strandlund for providing extra insight and a female perspective to a potentially testosterone-filled book.

Kem Meyer for writing the foreword and lending her name to the project.

Joe Cavazos for making the book look good.

You. For reading this book. I hope you were encouraged and challenged to make sure people feel very welcome in your church. As an extra bonus, your purchase of this book helps support the work of the nonprofit Center for Church Communication, which helps churches communicate better. If you found this book valuable, we hope you'll spread the word.